PLANNING IN ACTION

VISIONS AND REALITIES IN A COUNTRY TOWN

Honiton looking East

PLANNING IN ACTION
VISIONS AND REALITIES IN A
COUNTRY TOWN

by

Anne Glyn-Jones

Devon County Council and the University of Exeter

ISBN 0 85989 169 0

Printed by Short Run Press Ltd., Exeter, Devon

CONTENTS

LIST OF ILLUSTRATIONS AND MAPS

FOREWORD

This publication is the fifth in a series sponsored jointly by Exeter University and the Devon County Council. It is the product of a Research Fellowship held by Anne Glyn-Jones (MA *Oxon.*) which began in 1973. Each study has had a steering group of University academics and County Council senior staff appropriate to the topic.

First in the series was *Growing Older in a South Devon Town* (1975), devoted to Exmouth (1971 population around 26,000). The conclusions derived from the research had implications for local authorities, particularly in their social services, housing and environmental roles, as well as for voluntary bodies. The next four studies form a sequence examining the social and economic reasons for change alongside the statutory work of the Local Planning Authorities and their environmentally-based powers and duties. The aim has been to examine and record the various perceptions and actions at different times of those endeavouring in their respective fields to influence the social, economic and environmental changes in parts of Devon; and to put these in the context of the actual changes that have occurred. Thus the analyses have covered such intangibles as the evolution over time of the attitudes and opinions of significant groups, as well as such concrete matters as the actions taken and the statistical evidence of change so far as it can be quantified in terms of headcount and pounds sterling or acres. The starting date of the studies is approximately 1964 because in that year the first review of the statutory Devon Development Plan first set out environmental policies relating to the pattern of settlements.

Village into Town (1977) was a study of transition in south Devon. It examined over a 15-year period Ivybridge, a small town about 10 miles east of the centre of Plymouth. Initially a linear village astride a trunk road, with a 1961 population of about 1750, Ivybridge was selected in 1964 as a focus for development, with consequential implications for the rate and location of new development, as well as for its educational facilities and the bypassing of Trunk Road traffic. The County Council wanted an impartial analysis made as an aid to the assessment of corporate management techniques and, as a local newspaper said at the time, 'it got it'.

From the third investigation emerged *Rural Recovery: Has it Begun?* (1979) a study of Hatherleigh in north west Devon, some seven miles north of Okehampton on the northern edge of Dartmoor, a parish with a declining population that in 1971 was little over 900. The study examined what had been happening in Hatherleigh over the period in the context of the whole complex planning processes of the various statutory authorities, with particular reference to the parish's selection as a 'key' settlement. It found 'a rural microcosm where change is in the direction of more liveliness, more children and young adults and an influx of people managing to be economically self-supporting and, in most cases, content to have come. To a large extent these changes have occurred . . . as the result of personal choice and individual initiatives'. Included in the publication is an account of discussions on the report's findings at a seminar attended by over 50 people, both local residents and those with statutory responsibilities.

The fourth report was *Small Firms in a Country Town* (1982). Honiton, with about 5,000 population (1971), located some 16 miles east of Exeter, was chosen for this study, which concentrated on economic, particularly employment, change between 1961 and 1980. It shows the significance of small enterprises in a town which has enjoyed no special statutory assistance, and notes that the small business sector draws heavily on those who are deemed failures by the formal education system; furthermore, that most of what has happened has originated locally.

This, the fifth study, (1983) also considers Honiton, in the wider perspective of the decisions of various authorities between 1964 and 1980. As the introduction explains, Honiton was chosen because, though never an assisted area, 'it appeared to be changing rapidly and had been the subject of considerable interest, figuring in regional as well as local proposals'. Analysis of the 1981 census has suggested what was not evident when the work began — that it is the less remote rural areas, of which Honiton is an example, that may expect to be in the forefront of population increase in the immediate future. The main thrust of the study is concerned with the intertwined political and economic strands of the planning process rather than with the content of development control, either aesthetics or land use change. 'Between the idea and the reality', wrote T. S. Eliot in *The Hollow Men*, 'falls the shadow'. It is the area of the shadow that this work examines, and its perceptions are valid beyond the confines of one market town in Devon.

Although this study ends a sequence of four, it is intended that the Research Fellowship will continue to be used to illuminate what has happened, what is occurring and what may best be done to influence the future. The studies may well be relevant to similar situations either in the County or elsewhere, as well as to arguments in a general policy context. The University and the County Council have been fortunate in the selection of Anne Glyn-Jones as the Research Fellow, not only for the thorough groundwork and lively presentation of these investigations but also for the perceptive picture she gives of human endeavour in each case.

A confident approach to the future requires both Vision and Realism; the former has to be shared and sustained over a period and the latter has in due course to be demonstrated. By examining periods, generally of fifteen years, these studies help to show what this means for statutory authorities. Such enquiries offer no comfort to those who advocate even more detailed and centralised control by government, as they also demonstrate that change is the product of innumerable individual decisions mostly in pursuit of individual aims; and that, although authorities and official bodies can be given duties of a surprisingly comprehensive nature, they can only provide an acceptable framework for a time. The constructive activities of a large number of individuals are the main influences on the changes which occur.

David Macklin
Chief Executive
Devon County Council

William Ravenhill
Reardon Smith Professor of Geography
and Head of Department
University of Exeter.

ACKNOWLEDGEMENTS

This study ranges over a wide spectrum of statutory responsibilities, and help in its compilation has been equally widespread. Officers of East Devon District Council and of the South West Water Authority have advised, and I have been received with endless patience by the many officers of Devon County Council from whom I have sought information and help, particularly those in the Planning, Education, Social Services and Estates Surveyors Departments. Dr Terry Glanvill, a former Mayor of Honiton, also gave me most valuable assistance. Once again I have been guided by a Steering Committee composed, for this assignment, of Professor W. Ravenhill, Professor G. D. Mitchell, Dr M. Blacksell and Mr A. Gilg from Exeter University's Sociology and Geography Departments, and of Mr J. Hamson, Mr J. Owen and Mr P. Turnbull, directors of Devon County's Social Services, Education and Planning Departments respectively. To Mr Turnbull, now retired, I owe a special debt of gratitude for the many hours he has given to our discussions.

The Exeter *Express and Echo* kindly allowed me to use the three photographs on pages ii, 46 and 56 and I am indebted to the Ministry of Defence for the aerial photograph of Honiton. The remaining photos were taken by Andrew Teed of the University Geography Department staff. Terry Bacon, Geography Department, drew the maps.

I am also indebted to the University of Exeter Publications Committee, in particular its reader Dr J. H. Coates, for arranging the publication and distribution of this report.

Anne Glyn-Jones

I

INTRODUCTION

In the financial year 1948–49 Devon County Council for the first time instituted a Planning Committee and budgeted for a Planning Department. The legislation which engendered this new departure was the Town and Country Planning Act of 1947, the main purpose of which, as its preamble explained, was to make fresh provision for planning the development and use of land, for the granting of permission to develop land, and for other powers of control over the use of land. It required every local planning authority to carry out a survey of their area and submit a report, together with a plan, indicating the manner in which they proposed that land in their area should be used. The plan could in particular define the sites of proposed roads, public and other buildings and works, airfields, parks, pleasure grounds, nature reserves and other open spaces, or allocate areas of land for use for agricultural, residential, industrial or other purposes of any class specified in the plan. The Act also required the local authorities to designate land subject to compulsory purchase for various purposes.

The Ministry stipulated a vast list of subjects on which they required the collection of information for the survey.[1] The main headings cover

1 Existing land use; the age and condition of buildings, quantities of building uses; residential density; land unsuitable for building purposes.
2 Ancient monuments and buildings of architectural or historic interest.
3 Rural community structure.
4 Population — natural change and migration.
5 Industry and employment.
6 Minerals.
7 Agriculture and forestry.
8 Communications — roads, railways, docks, harbours and canals: airports and airfields.
9 Proposed developments by Government Departments.
10 Public utilities — water supply and sewerage; electricity; gas; land drainage.
11 Social services — education and health.

[1] Ministry of Town & Country Planning Circular No. 40 *Survey for Development Plans* 1948.

12 National parks, conservation and amenity areas.
13 Holiday development.

An Explanatory Memorandum from the Ministry of Housing and Local Government[1] stipulated that the plan should show 'which towns and villages are suitable for expansion and which can best be kept to their present size'. The County Map was to indicate what developments it was proposed should be carried out over the 20 years from 1951 to 1971, giving an indication of the time-scale in the hope of achieving co-ordinated public and private investment. All maps were due for submission to the Minister by July 1951. Like most Authorities, Devon, faced with the enormous amount of work involved, did not meet the deadline, but the plan was ready by 1952, at which point it was the Ministry which found itself over-worked, and the plan was not formally approved until 1959, seven years later.

The 1947 Act provided for a review to be made every five years from the date of approval. Since Devon's first plan, looking ahead to 1971, was not approved until 1959, the review was not made until 1964. The review looked ahead to 1981, was again caught in a backlog of work in Whitehall, and did not finally secure ministerial approval until 1971, again a seven-year span between submission and approval. A second review was undertaken in 1969, looking ahead to 1991. By then planning was operating under a new legislative umbrella, and as a result the Secretary of State did not give formal consideration to this review, although it formed the basis of planning decisions from its adoption in 1971 by the County Council.

In 1968 a new Planning Act incorporated proposals made by the Planning Advisory Group set up to assess the working of the planning system. County development plans had failed to adapt quickly enough to changing circumstances, and the Group proposed a separation of strategic from detailed tactical issues. The 1968 Act required the preparation of county structure plans, and provided for local plans to be prepared by local planning authorities, these local plans to conform to the overall policies promulgated in the structure plan. All were to be guided by over-arching regional strategies, for the delineation of which economic planning councils and boards had already (in 1964) been instituted throughout the country. Their task was primarily to promote economic growth. The structure plan process no longer involved, as did the old development plans, the preparation of a land-use map. The survey preceding the formulation of the plan was to identify the main social and economic features, and the plan itself was to pay particular attention to 'economic planning and the development of the region as a whole'. Instead of periodic five-year reviews, a system which had proved unworkable under the old legislation, the new Act required

[1] *Town and Country Planning Bill 1947 Explanatory Memorandum.* Cmd 7006 HMSO 1947.

constant monitoring of the survey material with the plan revised if and when the monitoring suggested it was necessary.

This study looks at how the central themes from these pivotal Acts worked out in practice in relation to one settlement — the market town of Honiton, in East Devon. Honiton was chosen because it appeared to be changing rapidly, and had been the subject of considerable interest, figuring in regional as well as local proposals. Three distinct but intertwined strands in the planning process come under review. One strand, which has been of increasing significance, is the political, focusing on those social or economic objectives held to be most pressing and important; and exploring the bounds of what is both realistic and acceptable. The second strand may be categorised as the management function, seeking to provide each of the various public services in the most appropriate way within the available resources — a task whose limitations must affect, and be affected by, the social and economic objectives of the political process. The third strand, defined by statute as Town and Country Planning, was established to regulate (via the mechanism of development control) changes in our physical environment, a concern which must respond to and may sometimes place constraints upon the objectives of the other two strands.

Important aspects of these three strands remain outside the study's scope. Honiton was never an assisted area to qualify for national financial aid for instance (see Figure 2), and although it was affected by national highways programmes in that a bypass was built round it, it was not well connected to the new south-west motorway, the M5, so that two of the major planning issues, the impact of regional assistance and of improved communications, are touched on only negatively; nor, in any case, are they subjects which could usefully be examined in relation to only one settlement. The study does not pursue in any depth the multifarious responsibilities of the planning system with regard to environmental protection, either as provided for in the 1947–1971 Planning Acts (covering the design of buildings, the preservation of trees, woodlands and buildings of special architectural or historical interest and giving powers of control over advertising); or the extensive initiatives of the 1949 National Parks and Access to the Countryside Act; or subsequent legislation on amenity and conservation areas. What is examined here is the continuing process of envisaging how one town's future might develop, together with an account of what action was possible with respect to encouraging private investment; and what considerations determined the direction and extent of public investment and the provision of statutory services. The study looks at the changes that have occurred in Honiton over some 15 years in the light of the evolving assumptions, expectations and aspirations (both local and from a wider context) which influenced the endeavour to shape the town's development. It examines foresight with hindsight.

3

II

A KEY INLAND TOWN

In the original Devon County Development Plan, Honiton was listed among 271 settlements (more than half of the total settlements identified in the Administrative County, i.e. excluding the then County Boroughs of Plymouth and Exeter) 'intended as centres for social, educational or health services'.

By the time of the first review, in the early 1960s, it was realised from the 1961 census that population in Devon was increasing by migration far faster than expected, but the overall increase was being accompanied by extensive rural depopulation, for people were congregating at the coast and particularly around Plymouth, Exeter and Torbay. This trend was unwelcome both because of the urban sprawl generated and because rural communities were becoming progressively more isolated, denuded, and expensive for the provision of statutory services.

The 1964 Development Plan set itself the goal of modifying this trend by concentrating rural resources on a limited number of focal points. There were to be two tiers: key settlements, to which new development would be directed and where an effort would be made to support a minimum range of services;[1] and above the key settlements in the hierarchy were to be key inland towns, which were to be developed as centres for rural communities 'within which a high standard of facilities and services may be concentrated' and where employment opportunities to replace agricultural employment 'may be best provided'.[2]

The selection of key inland towns depended on four criteria: (1) the existing possession of social capital the dissipation of which would not be justified; (2) the facilities and services provided and their accessibility as reflected by the size of their hinterlands; (3) their capacity for residential and industrial expansion; and (4) their relationship to adjacent towns, the objective being to concentrate resources and 'eliminate competing functions' — a somewhat strange ambition on the face of it, which presumably meant the avoidance of attempted provision of statutory services beyond the ability to sustain them.

Honiton met the criteria, one of 13 towns so designated, six of which were, like Honiton, in the 3,000 to 5,000 population range. (Two of the 13 were smaller, five larger.) In population size, Honiton had

[1] See A. Glyn-Jones, *Rural Recovery. Has it Begun?* for a discussion of the effectiveness of this policy in relation to the relatively remote key settlement of Hatherleigh in West Devon.
[2] *Analysis of Survey*, 1964 Devon County Council.

4

changed little over the decades, its principal *raison d'être* that of an agricultural market town. The lace trade for which it was once famous had declined, but the town's function as a reviver of travellers on the road from London into the West Country remained, with a multiplicity of hostelries fronting its wide and attractive main street. Population (see Appendix 1) rose gently from about 2,500 at the start of the nineteenth century to about 3,500 at the 1871 census, then declined rather more gradually and stood at about 3,000 in 1939. A war-time influx brought a population increase, and by the 1951 census, at which time there were about a thousand soldiers at the army camp on the edge of the borough, a total census population of some 4,600 was recorded.

Total numbers were only 100 higher at the 1961 census, but the proportion of servicemen was by then declining, so the figures conceal a probable increase of about 300 in the resident civilian population. Excluding the soldiers, the 1961 census gives an age breakdown (see Appendix 2) of 25.5. per cent under 16, 19.3 per cent of old age pensioners, and 55.2 per cent in the age groups in between. Compared with the average for Great Britain, this was a little above average for children, but the adults were more elderly than for Great Britain as a whole, where over 60 per cent were of working age, and less than 15 per cent old age pensioners.[1]

Within Honiton itself there was very little unemployment, and indeed in 1964 when Honiton became a key inland town the level of unemployment in the Honiton Employment Exchange Area (see Figure 2) was lower than the UK average — 1.5 per cent against 1.7 per cent (see Appendix 3). Honiton was nevertheless chosen, in line with the intentions of the settlement policy outlined above, as the site for one of the industrial estates which the County were in the process of establishing.

Devon had embarked on a programme of positive encouragement of industry in 1958, appointing an industrial development officer and seeking for suitable sites to offer industrialists. The proposal to attract industry to the County (which at that time of course excluded the County Boroughs of Exeter and Plymouth) and cease to rely on agriculture and tourism had initially been advanced to counter the migration of young people and the unemployment resulting from the decline in traditional primary industries. By the early 1960s it was realised that the movement of population into the County included not merely a retirement contingent but also a substantial proportion of people of working age. The 1964 plan accepted that employment generation needed to be on a scale to provide for migrants as well as

---

[1] Fifteen-year olds have been included among children, in order to make the statistics comparable with later usage, but prior to the raising of the school leaving age, 15-year olds would normally have counted as of working age.

local people — an argument which was disputed by conservationists who did not wish to see Devon built over, and who argued that if the job provision were not made, the population movement would not happen. The County Council took the view that planning neither could nor should negate the desire of people to move into Devon, but that it was part of the function of planning to accommodate the movement as satisfactorily as possible.

Attempts in the late 1950s to industrialise Devon were anything but encouraging. Widespread advertising had little effect. An Industrial Development Sub-Committee was set up in 1963, the advertising budget was increased, and a firm of advertising consultants engaged. The Sub-Committee obtained from the district councils information about 71 proposed industrial sites, and accepted 33 as satisfactory from the planning point of view. The County Council then decided to buy their own sites in what the 1964 version of the County Development Plan defined as regional centres and key inland towns, and thus it was that by 1964 three sites were under consideration in Honiton.

The choice fell on an area of land between the town and the new bypass being built to the north, but negotiations for the sale went badly and before the end of 1964 the Council decided to accelerate matters by designating the land for compulsory acquisition for industrial purposes, which required an amendment to the County Development Plan and therefore had to be submitted to the Minister of Housing and Local Government for approval. Many difficulties remained. The Ministry of Transport objected to the proposed access, and the proposals to satisfy them fell foul of Honiton Borough Council, for they involved the destruction of two valuable properties; and there were other objections which led to a public enquiry. In the end the County had to make a new access road, and these various delays meant that the proposed amendment first submitted to the Minister in July 1965 was not formally approved till April 1967. An industrialist was showing interest in the site, and the County's Estates Committee recommended that 42 acres be purchased for £43,000, on condition the firm concerned purchased from the County Council. The firm required an industrial development certificate (IDC), since Honiton was not an assisted area, and as time ticked by it was realised that if the certificate were not issued by early April the vendor would be involved in the development levy payable under legislation due to become operative on 6 April 1967. A special committee appointed to consider cases urgently affected by the Land Commission Act recommended acquiring the first 18 acres immediately, retaining an option over the other 24. The option has never been activated. Industry has been very slow to arrive, for reasons which will become apparent in this report.

Honiton Borough Council were firmly in favour of industrial development for their town, though discussions in Council during this

6

period were, to the irritation of some members, vague and generalised because, so they were informed, individual enterpreneurs did not wish to reveal their hand while negotiations were pending. Councillors also complained of lack of liaison with Devon County Council over the development of the County's estate, but in April 1966 they were informed that Wrigley's proposed to set up a major industrial enterprise in Honiton, employing about 300 people, for which they would acquire the entire county council estate and other land, and would erect a prestige factory, 'a beautiful factory in a beautiful setting'. Interviewing of potential employees would begin almost at once, and the firm asked for the Borough's help in providing interview rooms.

The total number of unemployed on the Honiton Employment Exchange Area (covering Honiton, Sidmouth and some 20 smaller settlements, see Figure 2) was at that time 153, including 139 men, 13 women and one girl. It was understandable therefore that Honiton's town clerk should, in informing his council members of Wrigley's impending arrival, comment 'We can but hope that the response to their advertisements is adequate'. The Clerk had been conducting a survey among firms who had toyed with, but rejected, the idea of coming to Honiton, and among four reported anonymously to the Council, one had remarked, referring to a disused factory up for sale in the town, 'It did seem to me that if the . . . factory is disposed of, it could absorb most of the available labour in Honiton, and I was therefore a little perturbed to find that you had in mind opening an industrial estate as well.' A second firm rejected Honiton because, however small the scale on which they opened any branch, they would expect to develop a factory of 35,000 square feet and a labour force of 300, which they regarded as their economically optimum size. They did not consider that Honiton offered the prospect of such a development. The other two firms were dissatisfied with the premises available (the disused factory), but in May the Borough were cheered to learn that a company proposed to buy the disused factory, and hoped in time to employ some 150 local people, building up to their maximum within 18 months to two years.

All now hinged on the IDC for Wrigleys. The question of IDCs for industry was much discussed between Devon County Council and the Board of Trade in the mid-1960s. The limit above which an IDC was required outside assisted areas was at the time 5000 square feet. Devon was insisting on the importance of factories in the 10,000 to 15,000 square feet range if there were to be job opportunities for school leavers, and they pressed, through the Joint Committee for the Economy of the South West, for greater flexibility in the issue of certificates. The Board initially held out little hope that certificates would be given in areas of Devon other than those with high unemployment such as Bideford or Brixham, but after further meetings Devon representatives came away

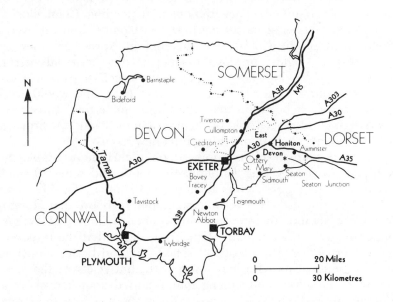

Fig. 1   Locations and Features mentioned in Text

Employment Exchange Areas within Devon showing dates of commencement of status

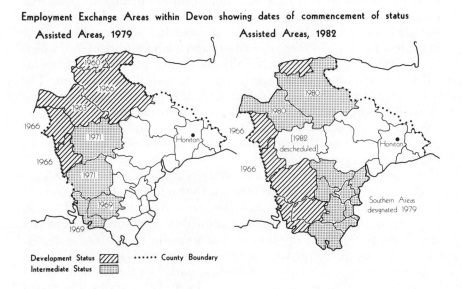

Fig. 2   Devon Assisted Areas, 1964–1980

8

with the impression that although no assurances had been given, prospects were not hopeless.

Discussions about Wrigley's IDC continued for over a year, meanwhile the County's negotiations to amend the County Development Plan and acquire the industrial site were also proceeding. In June 1967 the blow fell. The Board of Trade advised the company that they would not grant an IDC. The reasons given, according to the company, were that another firm was proposing to move to Honiton and employ 150 of the small local labour force; and that the size and prospective growth of Wrigley's enterprise was unsuitable for the resources of the area.

There was an explosion of wrath from Honiton, and widespread suggestions that the company were, for political reasons connected with a by-election, being put under pressure to go to Plymouth, which was also, at that time, not an assisted area, though future unemployment was expected as a result of a run-down of the dockyards. The nature of this pressure was believed, as evidenced in the Borough Minutes, to include false information given to the company, such as the suggestion that Exeter Airport was to close, and proposed railway freight connections with Exeter to be abandoned. Whatever the truth, had the Wrigley development gone ahead at Honiton, it would have made the town heavily vulnerable to the fortunes of a single industry. The disadvantages of operations which are large-scale, at least in relation to their particular environmental circumstances, is illustrated by another aspect of this story, the Board of Trade's explanation that the proposed new entrepreneur with his projected 150 employees would pre-empt the local labour market. This enterprise did not develop to the extent forecast and did not require the numbers envisaged. Wrigley's, however, did become a substantial employer of Plymouth labour, and the outcome was probably for the best.

As Honiton's Clerk was not slow to point out, everyone had wasted a year, and in addition the new rates to be generated would accrue to Plymouth not to the Administrative County. Devon's Industrial Development Sub-Committee pursued the matter with the Board of Trade, but to no avail. All that could be done was to begin again.

The Board of Trade had indicated that they were not opposed in principle to industry at Honiton provided it was of the 'right' size. This was a matter which the Clerk to Devon County Council said he would elucidate with the Board, but if any answer was received, documentary evidence has not survived the 1974 local government re-organisation. Meanwhile, the County continued its slow progress towards establishing the estate. The cost for the 18 acres was now budgeted at £35,000 for the land, plus £60,000 for roads etc.

In 1969 half the site was disposed of to the Express Dairy, who found themselves short of space at their existing works some seven miles away at Seaton Junction. Much of their existing workforce already lived in

Honiton. In the same year work began on new premises for an engineering firm which was outgrowing the premises in Honiton where it had spent the previous ten years. Neither firm could be regarded as migrating industry. No further developments occurred for the next five years.

III

THE SEARCH FOR GROWTH

The interest in attracting industry to Devon underwent a transformation during the 1960s, one that was to dominate planning attitudes for a decade. The mission of the Joint Committee for the Economy of the South West, set up in January 1963 including representatives from the Counties of Cornwall, Devon, Somerset and Dorset, and the County Boroughs of Plymouth and Exeter, was to pursue measures for combating unemployment. Following pressure from this Committee, the Government agreed to put up half the cost of an economic survey of the South West to be conducted by an independent consultancy — Associated Industrial Consultants.

The resulting report, *The Economic and Industrial Development of the South West*, was presented in March 1965. It was compiled at a time when both parties vying to form the government at the 1964 general election were putting great emphasis on economic growth, and were promising expansion of around four per cent per annum. The report took little interest in the unemployment issue to which it owed its genesis, indeed it remarked that industry was short of both skilled and unskilled labour. What pre-occupied the consultants was the evidence they found of 'under-utilised resources', including, in the South West as a whole, some 130,000 persons of working age not at work, as evidenced by low activity rates. Some of these, they admitted, might have retired early, or be in 'concealed' employment in agriculture or the holiday trade, but the likelihood was that many women were simply not looking for work. They suspected that the active work force, too, was not sufficiently diligently occupied, and under-employment was suspected 'in terms of part-time working, temporary employment and self-employment'. The cure for these and other ills (such as excessive employment dependency on Plymouth dockyard) was 'balance', which meant getting the proportion of people working in industry (17 per cent in the Devon case) up closer to the national average (38 per cent). In addition to its distrust of part-timers and the self-employed, the report criticised the local economy for the high numbers of smaller-then-average farms, and commented adversely on the number of small firms employing less than 20 people. It further pointed out that 'the present availability of industrial sites is inadequate for the necessary programme of industrial development'.

Devon County Council was well aware of the problem of industrial sites. Although the difficulty over obtaining IDCs persisted, by the autumn of 1965 the advertising campaign to attract industry had to be temporarily suspended because of the shortage of sites. Unfortunately the Ministry of Housing and Local Government had asked councils to defer 'non-essential' capital projects, and the purchase of land in advance of requirements. An attempt was made to get Devon MPs to press for special loan sanction for further site purchases — one of many recurring examples of the impact of resource realities on policy proposals.

The Minutes of Devon's Planning Committee, to whom a very full summary of the AIC report was despatched, merely record laconically that it was 'received'.

While so far as the County's deliberations were concerned the AIC report was apparently left to gather dust, at the national level a parallel set of ideas was being promulgated in the new Labour Government's National Plan, which was published in September of the same year, 1965. The target of a 25 per cent growth in national output between 1964 and 1970 postulated an increase in the demand for labour of 800,000 over the plan period. The likely increase in available manpower was put at about 400,000, a calculation based on population projections pre-dating the immigration controls introduced in 1962, and relying on continuing immigration to fulfil even this half-target. For the next quarter-target of 200,000, the Plan sought to bring into productive activity older people whom the spread of pension schemes had tempted into retirement, and women, particularly some of the three million married women aged 45 to 65 who were not in the paid labour force.

The Plan admitted that activity rates were higher in 1965 than at the peak of war-time mobilisation in 1943, but there were regional variations, and the Plan pointed out that if the regions with the lowest rates could be brought up to the average, another 319,000 people could be brought into the labour force. The Plan settled for the assumption that these various measures would produce a total increase of 600,000, leaving the equivalent of the remaining 200,000 to be achieved by increased productivity.

The relevance of all this to the South West was twofold. First, the region was noted, as the AIC report had already pointed out, for 'one of the lowest activity rates in the country, and a large potential reserve of labour'. Secondly, there was relatively low population density in the South West, for, said the Plan, 'the immediate problem of securing faster growth is closely related to the longer-term problem of securing a more balanced regional development of industry and housing in the context of a rapidly growing population. On present forecasts, the population of the United Kingdom will grow by 20 million over the rest of the century'.

This was the climate of opinion in which Devon commissioned its next report. In the spring of 1966 an independent industrial consultant had proposed that the Tamar river would be an appropriate area for a major petro-chemical complex of industries. In March Devon County Council again commissioned AIC, asking them to assess 'the range of industries that might be introduced or developed in Devon and Plymouth' and 'the feasibility of developing within the area a group of industries associated with one or more primary producer industries'.

The resulting report, *Industry and Growth*, submitted in August 1966, did not content itself with its immediate objectives any more than its predecessor had done. The first AIC report had, like the National Plan of the same year, made much of the under-utilised resources of labour in the South West, recommending the introduction of manufacturing to mop them up. The second report, presented in September 1966, lost confidence that the labour would actually allow itself to be mopped up. The low activity rates which had seemed so persuasive the previous year were now re-appraised in the light of 'factors which suggest that this does not indicate a major source of untapped labour'. The factors were the same as those mentioned in the earlier report — i.e. large numbers of early-retired people, and seasonal work in tourism and farming; but the interpretation now was that these people would not volunteer to work in industry, nor did the notionally unemployed promise much better a response, for 'substantial numbers . . . will move into the holiday trade [at the end of the winter] and others . . . are occupational pensioners'.

The report therefore concentrated on the other relevant aspect of the National Plan: population growth and regional imbalance. The big conurbations were held to be bursting at the seams — London needed to get rid of a million people by 1980. The obvious solution, according to the reports, was for Devon to embark upon a vigorous policy of population growth. Only by demonstrating its determination and ability to identify its own local interests with those of the country at large could Devon hope to attract from National Government the sort of funding that would be necessary to get roads, hospitals and other medical facilities and improved services.

The consultants considered four approaches. They rejected both the idea of a New Town and the suggestion for a series of small expansions in a large number of centres. They recommended the expansion of existing (major) centres and of smaller centres clustered round and dependent on a major centre. They recommended three major phases of expansion. The last should deal with Tavistock and North Devon; the intermediate one with the development of Totnes, Newton Abbot, Crediton and Cullompton; and the first priority should be the injection, within ten years, of 25,000 to the Plymouth/Ivybridge area, 20,000 in the Honiton area, and 5,000 at Barnstaple, (which was in the North Devon Development Area). The Honiton development was described as 'a logical next major step in the direction west from London via Basingstoke – Andover – North Dorset, and south from Severnside via Taunton'. Feasibility studies should be started at once in the Plymouth and Honiton areas. Negotiations should be opened with exporting authorities to attract planned additional population, and a campaign should begin to attract family migration. In describing this report to the Industrial Development Sub-Committee, Devon's Clerk remarked that the fundamental issue it raised was the need for growth in manufacturing coupled with arrangements for population of the right age group to be deliberately attracted into the County.

The suggestion for 'planned migration' was not novel. The proposal to enter into 'overspill' arrangements under the terms of the Town Development Act of 1952 as a method of stimulating economic development had been suggested, in particular, by Tiverton, but at the time Devon was thought to be too far from potential exporting authorities. Early in 1966 however, notwithstanding the distrust of some county councillors for the whole prospect of planned migration, the County, in conjunction with the local authorities concerned, authorised feasibility studies in both Tiverton and Barnstaple. There were local objections, and demands that the final decision be the subject of a referendum, demands which the County's officers resisted on the grounds that the elected representatives should speak for their areas. In the event, the Barnstaple feasibility study was followed late in 1967 by a referendum which rejected the overspill proposals by nearly three votes to one, whereupon the Borough Council terminated its interest in overspill negotiations, and the County Council took no further action to pursue a town development scheme for Barnstaple.

This outcome still lay in the future when district representatives, in November 1966, met with county councillors and officers to discuss the second AIC report. It was evident that there were widespread differences of view. Both among the county and the district represen-tatives there was support for the rejected fourth proposal — small-scale growth at a large number of small centres. 'Small businesses should be given a chance.' The representatives of Honiton Rural District in particular expressed the view that it was better to encourage small business and let it grow up with the problems absorbed as it went along rather than 'take a big problem into our midst'. The planners firmly advised against the fourth proposal, however, as inefficient and uneconomic in the provision of 'schools, health services, sewage disposal, gas and electricity supplies' – the argument to which the county councillors had already acceded in accepting the settlement policy embodied in the 1964 review of the County Development Plan. The various county committees all considered the AIC report and accepted its recommendations to begin feasibility studies.

Honiton Municipal Borough councillors were untypical of the

14

district level of local government in welcoming the prospects of planned expansion. In August 1966 they had been alerted by press reports to the proposed expansion of their town, then numbering about 4,400 civilians and 700 soldiers, by some 20,000 people within 10 years, and were disappointed, when they learnt the full details at the meeting in November, that the recommendation concerned the Honiton – Tiverton – Exeter triangle, not necessarily Honiton itself. They were somewhat concerned at the proposed time-scale, which required, so the report estimated, the building of 590 houses annually for 10 years. The number of new houses over the previous five years had totalled only about 120.

In March 1967 representatives of both Honiton Rural District and the Municipal Borough went to County Hall to discuss the proposed feasibility study for their area. At the same time was published the South West Economic Planning Council's study *Region with a Future*[1] The regional planning boards and councils were set up by the new Labour Government of 1964, as part of the apparatus associated with the National Plan. They existed for 15 years, until abolished by the Conservatives in 1979. Their purpose included helping Britain

> to achieve an increase in output that is faster and more evenly spread than in the past. They seek to draw into productive use untapped labour reserves and to speed up the expansion of output in those regions where it is slower than elsewhere. The aim is a full and balanced development of the country's economic and social resources. A major factor of which to take account in national and regional planning is the expected increase in the country's population. . . .[2]

The values exemplified, the statistics used, the assumptions made and the goals specified being the same as in the AIC's *Industry and Growth*, SWEPC's *Region with a Future* naturally came to the same conclusions, albeit for broader areas since the SWEPC brief extended from the Scillies to Gloucestershire. Crucial to the whole argument was the following:

> Planned migration of peoples and of industries to give them employment could become a major factor in the economic development of the South West. . . . The problems of London and other conurbations are urgent.

So far as the Honiton area was concerned, SWEPC's conclusions were:

> The Exeter–Torbay sub-division would benefit from industrial development to the north and east of Exeter as well as at Plymouth. The local planning authorities concerned are studying the feasibility of a planned overspill scheme in the Tiverton area, between Exeter and Taunton, and intend to study similarly the Honiton and Exeter areas. The Council

[1]*Region with a Future* A draft strategy for the South West. HMSO, 1967.
[2]*Economic Planning in the Regions, HMSO, 1966.*

hope these studies will yield positive results which will then be turned quickly into action.

. . . The Council invite urgent discussion of these choices for the future shape of the economies of the Southern and Western sub-regions. The Council intend to call upon the local planning authorities and regional interests concerned to work out a co-operative undertaking to make the most immediate use of the studies now in hand and to see what further local effort is required and may be best organised.

The planning councils, to which the civil servants of the planning boards reported, were appointed not elected. They included academics, businessmen, trade unionists, and members drawn from among both officers and councillors of local government. Their status, derived from their association with the National Plan, enjoyed more prestige than that of a private consultancy like AIC, and they could hope that their recommendations would feed directly into the Government's decisions on resource allocation for regional support. Their views were not mandatory, but could hope to benefit from strong advocacy within Devon, since both the Chairman of the County Council and the County Planning Officer served on the SWEPC. When the County Council came to discuss the proposals, they were firmly warned that their best chance of getting any government help for infrastructure was to co-operate in accepting population from over-crowded areas.

Doubts were not thereby stilled. A motion that large-scale overspill would not benefit Devon was deflected to the Planning Committee for further consideration. There was considerable opposition to the overspill proposals outside the ranks of councillors also, and during the summer of 1967 Honiton Borough Council was lobbied by the Overspill Resistance Association. Honiton's Town Clerk in November of 1967 put before his Council some of the problems involved, quoting an MP who had said, 'if in the next decade we are to uproot hundreds of thousands of city-dwellers and in the process upset millions of country people, we need to make sure, in advance, that the results are going to be worth it. Overspill *can* be successful; but only if it solves more problems than it creates.' The problems of which the Clerk warned included the possibility that housing would outrun the provision of services and employment. Would the Board of Trade issue IDCs for industry, would the Ministry of Health produce the clinics and maternity services? What about schools? Children's playgrounds? Could 20,000 new people be integrated with the existing 5,000? Would the expansion pay for itself in terms of increased rates, or would new expenditure outstrip income?

Town expansion appealed to the Council. The Borough's decision, late in 1967, was that an ultimate total population of between 15,000 and 20,000 would be acceptable if achieved over a reasonable period.

'Reasonable', in this context, begged a good many questions. It was taken to mean 'such a period of time as will enable incoming population to be integrated with existing population and the provision in step with the population increase of the necessary public utilities (such as gas, water, electricity and sewerage) and social services (such as schools, clinic, medical and hospital services, recreational and cultural facilities, internal transport, and the needs of religion) and adequate opportunities for full employment.' With this perhaps somewhat utopian vision they awaited the feasibility study.

Completed in the summer of 1968, this study posed three choices — to allow Honiton to grow without active intervention; to encourage development; or to adopt a town development scheme. Honiton was in any case growing, partly, the study opined, because development was in fact already being encouraged by such county policies as the restriction of building at the coast, the selection of Honiton as a key inland town and the provision of the industrial estate (though in fact no outside industry had yet been attracted to it). But in view of the Government's preference for firms to move to Development Areas and to New and Expanding towns, it seemed probable that Honiton would not attract firms unless a town development scheme were instituted which 'would ally the aid of Government'. The study explained the mechanisms for instituting such a scheme and added an appendix listing, with details of housing and factories, all such schemes operating in England. It spelt out the administrative, demographic and financial ramifications involved. It concluded with an analysis of the potential limitations to growth, under the three categories of
1) the physical limitations, in terms of gradients, flood liability, and the preference for absorbing the least productive agricultural land first;
2) the provision of essential services: water, gas, sewerage, electricity;
3) the highway system.
There was also a subsidiary and variable limitation, and that was the size of the Army camp on the west of the Borough, where major changes in the number of troops and their families would react on the numbers by which the town might otherwise expand.

The study reckoned that at 25,000 the absolute limit would be reached from the point of view of river pollution and sewage effluent, and to reach such a number would require a new bulk electricity supply point. But short of that figure a number of other inhibitions occurred. If the best agricultural and wood land were to be saved, 20,000 was the maximum that could be accommodated, and that, pre-supposing an increase of 15,000, would require a new sewage works. An increase of 12,000 would mean reinforced electricity supplies, 10,000 more people would require new water supplies, 5,000 more would mean new gas supplies, and even 1,500 more would overload the existing sewage works. There was an additional limitation — the new bypass running

17

north of the town. If new development were to avoid crossing beyond the bypass, then 15,000–16,000 was the most who could be accommodated — an increase of 10,000 to 11,000. Growth on that scale would necessitate a full-scale town centre study. The final recommendation was that the maximum convenient size now envisaged be about 15,000, though the town could grow to about 20,000 in time.

The study then turned to the question of the time scale. Some 87 new houses had been built in 1966, but the study assumed that the building industry could build 500 to 600 new houses per year in Honiton if required. A projection of trends over the previous five years suggested an influx of 1,400 people by 1981, but faster growth might be expected as a result of policies deflecting development from the coast, and an influx of up to 3,000 might occur by 1981. The study considered the implications of a town development scheme not in the context of the ten-year crash programme recommended by AIC, but in the context of a 40-year development to 2010, with the comments

> To ensure that Honiton is able to continue its industrial and population growth after a town development scheme is undertaken the capacity of the town area should not be reached until the end of a longer period. Town development schemes have been studied within a 40 year context to the year 2010. This has the merit of coinciding with the estimated period during which car ownership will reach a point where all those wanting one will have one, so that this factor can be fully considered at the same time as the town area would be fully developed.

The implication of this was that the town's growth by 15,000 to a total of about 20,000 would take place over 40 years. The study reckoned that an intake of about 400 people annually could be assimilated without social disruption, and various ways of arranging the intake period are then discussed, with graphs and tables analysing natural increase, normal migrational increase with extra retirement migration, and the effect of three different sorts of agreement with the Greater London Council assuming intake periods to 1981 or 1985. Influences already operative could be expected to produce a total population (including troops) of about 15,000 by 2010, and the other proposals would produce from 16,750 to 22,950. The implications of this in speed and location of land take-up are then explored; the requirements for retail shops and their expected turnover; the impact on local administration, social services, transport and telephones (all of which would, and easily could, expand); and on Exeter's ample provision of hospital services and further education facilities. An analysis of employment prospects assumed that, though jobs in agriculture would be lost to urban development, firms coming in as part of the scheme would provide jobs as needed by the new population, and there was some discussion of the social integration of newcomers, among whom persons born in Ireland

18

or the New Commonwealth were not expected to constitute proportions very different from those already in Honiton.

In dealing with the financial aspects, the study looked at the extra provision of office, police, library and other requirements which the County would have to provide, and concluded that 'the effect on the county rate would be less than 1d rate increase'. Rents on houses provided under a scheme would have to be higher than in present Honiton council houses, which might lead to a decision to equalise rents ('subject to the protection of individual tenants under the rebate scheme') and the need for sewerage expenditure would put up rates initially before the increase in population occurred. On balance 'Increased expenditure will be incurred in providing the usual district council services required for the expanded population. In general, however, these costs will be met by the increased rateable resources which will accrue with every addition in population.' No financial loss was expected to accrue to the local authority from any transactions in the provision of industrial sites and little risk in transactions over residential land, unless the 'programme rate' were not realised.

The conclusion was that present trends would produce a 1981 population of about 8,000, which could be enhanced to either 9,650 or 11,550 by a different scale of town development scheme. Such a growth would generate prosperity, and not put excessive strains on either the financial or other resources of the local authorities.

In October 1968 the study was put on sale to the public, following a meeting at which county and district representatives jointly 'received' the report. The Borough Council began arrangements for local consultations and meetings, inviting GLC representatives to attend. Late in October the Borough Council adopted the highest of the proposals, and decided to promote a town development scheme designed to achieve a population of 11,550 by 1981.

In coming to this conclusion, the Honiton Borough Council was departing from the more typical reactions of Devon local authorities. Barnstaple had rejected by a referendum the proposal for an 'overspill' agreement, and during 1968 both Tiverton Rural District Council and Tiverton Borough Council reached similar conclusions following feasibility studies in their areas. Devon County Council was itself passing to and fro between committees the motion (arising out of the SWEPC report) which invited the Council to declare 'its conviction that large scale migration of London overspill population into the county and the creation of any new town for their reception would not benefit the people of Devon and should be resisted' — a motion which Devon County Council were to adopt in April 1969.[1] It must have been

[1] At the time Devon County Council adopted this resolution, Honiton was still maintaining a rather desultory contact with the GLC, and, on the passage of the resolution, became uncertain whether they could any longer count on the support of the County if they pursued an overspill

some consolation to the hardworking study teams that Honiton did not come to such a conclusion.

Within the week in which Honiton made its bold decision, word was received from the GLC that they were not at present interested in entering into any new town development schemes. Undeterred, the Borough applied to the Ministry of Housing and Local Government for suggestions of other potential population-exporting authorities, but the Ministry had no suggestion to make. The Borough approached Birmingham Corporation, Manchester, Bristol and Liverpool, but received negative or at least discouraging replies from all. Birmingham commented that in their experience industry was unwilling to move with the people; and Manchester also commented on their unhappy experience of moving families who could find no work in the new area, and returned to Manchester. They added that 'it would be up to Honiton to sell Honiton to the industrialists. . . . it should not be assumed that there is much large scale industry in Manchester on the move . . .'. Liverpool doubted if they could persuade people to go as far as Devon — adding 'there is difficulty in persuading people to go even as far as Burnley'. Bristol had to report that its housing situation had eased and there was difficulty in 'nominating suitable applicants for overspill'. Only Manchester and the GLC held out hope that the matter might be worth pursuing in the future.

The Ministry of Housing and Local Government proposed to hold discussions with the County and District Council about the implications of the studies for the future development of the County and SWEPC welcomed the Honiton study and looked forward to the Exeter area study, to which the indefatigable study team were now free to devote their attention. SWEPC also proposed to involve themselves in discussions of the regional implications of the study.

There was thus no lack of studious application to the prospects of industrial development. Honiton Council kept in touch with the GLC in the hope of a change of policy, and meanwhile turned their attention to the topic which had figured so prominently in the replies from the urban authorities — the development of the industry which was to provide jobs for the increasing local population.

---

scheme. On seeking reassurance, they were told that the Planning Committee would be happy to discuss the matter further, but the actual decision lay with the District. At the end of 1969 the Borough Clerk reported that further discussions with the GLC suggested that a scheme sometime in the future might be a possibility. But in fact nothing came of it, though it was not until 1976 that the GLC formally rescinded its over-successful attempts to shed population.

IV

ASSESSING THE FUTURE

Planned migration or no planned migration, people were moving to Honiton. The 1964 review of the County Development Plan had envisaged, on the basis of past experience, that population would reach 4,830 by 1981.[1] By the end of 1967 the assessment of current population, based on housing completions, had reached 4,600 and was increasing by 100 per year (see Appendix I). This was held to be partly due to 'increased demand arising from Ministry of Defence requirements', presumably houses for soldiers' families, but in addition the county planners detected a deflection to inland towns of demand from those seeking homes in East Devon but deterred by coastal prices. In the succeeding two years the speed of development increased. Housing completions (see Appendix 4) reached a crescendo in 1967–68, with 185 private and 107 local authority houses completed, compared with combined totals of 21, 75 and 91 in the preceding three years. The civilian population estimate was up by almost a thousand by 1970, to 5,500. As things turned out this was a considerable over-estimate, for the 1971 census showed only just over 5,000. The following ten years added a further 1,500, with the 1981 census producing a civilian figure of just over 6,500.

The rapidity of change and of supposed change in the late Sixties had implications for three areas of public policy. What investment should be made for the provision of statutory services? What provision could be made for employment? What assumptions should be fed into the formal planning machinery? The relationship between these three considerations is not as close as might be expected.

The formal planning machinery was affected at two levels. There were the long-term studies, feeding into revisions of the County Development Plan and later into the Structure Plan; and there were the local plans for use in development control. From 1968 until the Structure Plan of 1979 there were five major published studies incorporating the Honiton area, two plans at the strategic level, and two local plans plus a town centre study (see Appendix 9). The expected level of population affected all of them.

Population forecasts for Honiton were always somewhat bedevilled

[1] Presumably civilians, including soldiers' families, since the 1961 figure with which this estimate is compared is not the 1961 census figure (4,718 including troops) but the Registration-General's mid-year estimate (4,020) of *civilian* population.

21

by the presence of the Army camp, where the number of soldiers had varied from less than a hundred to over 1,000. The totals had relevance to, for instance, sewage decisions, but not to employment. In fact the camp closed in 1971, but in any case, as population projections increased, its impact on total numbers diminished. The Honiton feasibility study of 1968 had postulated a 1981 population of 8,000, even in the absence of a town development scheme, a figure which translated into an assessment for 1,000 to 2,000 new houses over the years 1969–1981.

During 1969 both the *Exeter and District Joint Feasibility Study* and the second review of the *County Development Plan* appeared. The Honiton feasibility study had in effect not been able to support the AIC suggestion for 20,000 to be settled within 10 years but had thought that 15,000 might be introduced over the 40 years to 2010. The *Exeter and District Joint Feasibility Study*, produced in the knowledge that no town development scheme was probable, nevertheless drew on the evidence of rapid unplanned migration to suggest that Honiton might by 2010 absorb 10,000 of an expected intake for the study area of 106,900. The *Analysis of Survey* for the second review, calculating that the Honiton study's 8,000 by 1981 might be on the high side, plumped for that figure not to be reached until 1991. It was also in 1969 that the County and the Borough agreed on an outline development plan for Honiton, which when first presented to the Borough for signature in 1966 had allowed for a 1981 population of 4,830, but by 1969 postulated 6,350. Three years later, in 1973, a revised Honiton outline development plan (agreed in 1974) improved on the *Analysis of Survey* by anticipating a population for Honiton of 10,000 in 1991, largely as a result of coastal deflection.

Two years later a second SWEPC Study, *A Strategic Settlement Pattern for the South West*, made a fresh population assessment and introduced a new round of localised studies, rather as the AIC report had instigated the feasibility studies welcomed in the first SWEPC report of 1967. The county development plans had been prepared under the requirements of the Labour Government's 1947 Town and Country Planning Act. Their 1968 Town and Country Planning Act, confirmed in the Conservative Government's 1971 Town and Country Planning Act, replaced county development plans by structure plans 'formulating the local planning authority's policy and general proposals in respect of the development and other use of land in that area . . .'. This was to be undertaken by county councils 'having regard to current policies with respect to the economic planning and development of the region as a whole . . .'.

SWEPC's new strategy began by saying that although, under the 1968 Act, structure plans were the responsibility of local authorities, the Secretary of State for the Environment was anxious 'to see the earliest

22

publication of regional strategies . . . providing . . . the framework for regional development, transportation and planning. Accordingly we are presenting this strategic report to give the regional context to guide the local planning authorities in the South West in carrying out their statutory planning responsibilites.'

This revised strategy for the South West was a modest document compared with its predecessor, both in its length and in its self-assessment. Its thesis was that population in the South West had increased more swiftly than in the nation at large, was likely to continue to do so, and that this posed problems, particularly in so attractive an area, over where to site both the people and the infrastructure to support them. 'The starting point for our strategy' it stated 'is our judgement about the implications of existing trends for the size of the regional population at the end of the century, and experience has shown that population projections can prove very wrong. A long-term view is nevertheless necessary.' Though recognising that 'long-term population forecasting is always hazardous', the report was prepared to be specific. Of the Exeter/East Devon Area (Economic Planning Area 14 in the transitory parlance of the SWEPC) the Council expressed concern that 'the distinctive characteristics of the environment should be conserved' but in assessing that recent trends would add 90,000 by the end of the century, they merely commented 'there seems little doubt that growth of this magnitude will occur'. They approved existing policies of coastal restraint, and hoped for 'the accommodation of most of this large growth inland along the Exeter–Tiverton axis, making the assumption that this can be accomplished without undue depreciation of this area's high environmental and agricultural quality'.

Thus in 1975 there were three current assessments of population growth in East Devon, all with differing geographical boundaries. The *Exeter and District Joint Feasibility Study* had postulated an increase of 106,900 by 2010, an increase of 43.4 per cent over the 44 years 1966 to 2010. The second review of the *County Development Plan* had projected its figures for East Devon minus Exeter (then a County Borough) and had forecast an addition of 45,000 by 1991, an increase of 29.4 per cent in the 23 years 1968 and 1991. Now SWEPC chose an intermediate date of 2001, and its forecast of a 90,000 increase over the 30 years 1971–2001 yielded a 32.7 per cent increase (EPA14, covering Exeter and East Devon, included parts of East Devon on the Dorset border omitted from the Exeter study, which had concentrated on parishes thought to be within commuting distance of Exeter).

These figures had been discussed with the pre-1974 Devon County Council, whose officers had warned that with the opening of the M5 motorway the figures might prove too low. In the light of the intention to preserve the coast, the main issue raised was whether to try to accommodate the increase round Exeter, or to disperse it more widely.

One thing was certain — and the Council so resolved: it was not possible to accommodate the growth of population proposed for Exeter and East Devon without substantial amendment to the County Development Plan. They bequeathed to the new Devon County Council a resolution that 'the County Council wholly reserves its position pending further consultation and consideration of what amendment would be involved', to which was rapidly appended the further resolution that 'this Council is totally opposed to the creation of new towns'.

At first sight this reaction seems surprising, for in terms of the rate of change implied, the average annual increase was greatest in the *County Development Plan* second review. The explanation no doubt is that when similar increases are postulated for the population within Exeter County Borough (not included in the Administrative County's Plan), it becomes obvious that many of these extra thousands could not be squeezed within the city boundaries but would have to find homes in the territory of the old County. The 1969 *Exeter and District Joint Feasibility Study*, made in conjunction with the city authorities, had made just such provision, proposing additional population capacity beyond trend expectations for various East Devon settlements and even concluding 'it is essential not to wait until it is too late before attempting to undertake the development of a major new settlement'. This of course rests on the assumption that if acceptable land provision for city expansion could not be made, the migrants projected to come to Exeter would be attracted to a rural settlement in East Devon in preference to an urban home elsewhere.

The new post-1974 Devon County Council were equally unhappy about the projections, and expressly dissociated themselves from the hope, expressed by the SWEPC Chairman, that the Secretary of State for the Environment 'will feel able to endorse our conclusions'. The County Council were to be disappointed, for the Secretary of State did endorse the report.

Work had now to begin, as legislation required, on Devon's first Structure Plan, to which SWEPC's analysis was intended as a contribution. As a start, the new Council had agreed that the Plymouth and Exeter areas should be the subject of sub-regional studies. Among the local authorities involved in the Exeter study was the East Devon District Council, into which the district responsibilities of the old Honiton Borough Council had been subsumed in the 1974 re-organisation. Like the old Honiton Borough Council, EDDC was temperamentally expansionist, and, with strong representation from Exmouth, Sidmouth and the other coastal towns, enunciated planning principles critical of the policies of coastal restraint which SWEPC, like the County Council, wished to see encouraged.

The new Exeter study, *Towards 2001 — The Future of the Exeter Sub-*

24

Region, had for purposes of consultation whittled the options for settling the population increase down to six:
1) to let existing trends continue;
2) to concentrate facilities in linked though more remote settlements;
3) to let the main emphasis be on the coastal towns;
4) to emphasize the inland towns;
5) to emphasize both the inland and the coastal towns;
6) to concentrate on Exeter and the Exe Valley.

East Devon District Council expressed a preference for options 2, 4 and 5, and these were the options selected in the study for public canvas.

By the time this study was in preparation, demographic trends were suggesting a re-appraisal of SWEPC's population forecasts. Birth-rate changes alone had resulted in a drop from 90,000 to 77,000 in the expected increase. Within this framework, a series of assumptions were made about the possible age composition of the up-to-70,000 new population, and the differing housing, employment, sport and recreational needs which might result. Tables revealed how these assessments would be distributed over the existing settlements according to the revised selected options:

Option 1: the linked communities at a distance from Exeter, with two focal points, one for the north and one for the east of the area;

Option 2: inland town development, with Exeter dominant;

Option 3: inland and coastal development, again with Exeter dominant;

Honiton, of course, featured in all three options. Rather surprisingly, since trends within Honiton had already led, as recorded above, to a projected increase to 10,000 by 1991, this sub-regional study stated that the 1961–71 trend would produce only 1,000 extra in Honiton by 2001, giving an end-of-century total of 6,000 compared with the latest 1971 census figure of 5,000 odd. (Figures since then had suffered distortion because of the use of Honiton camp for Asian refugees from Uganda.) The explanation appears to be that the total increase to 2001 was taken, by definition, as 77,000, and this figure was then disaggregated over the settlements in such proportions as their respective rates of increase bore to one another in 1961–71. The options canvassed were intended to control the trends. Option 3, the dispersal of the expected 77,000 over inland and coastal towns resulted in a lower proposed figure for Honiton in 2001 (9,000), than was already proposed for 1991 in Honiton's own outline development plan (10,000). Option 2 produced the figure of 10,000 in Honiton in 2001 instead of by 1991. Option 1, however, proposed Honiton as a focal point for the development of the east of the study area, with a population of 12,000 by the end of the century, this option being designed to move the 'dominant triangle of economic activity' away from Exeter/Teignmouth/Sidmouth to Exeter/Tiverton/Honiton.

During the process of public consultation, the responses were so

25

varied that no one option took preference — districts tending to Option 3, parishes to Option 1. Honiton Parish Council preferred 1, the idea of dispersed but linked settlements; EDDC's preferred option was, not surprisingly, the third, with its emphasis on coastal as well as inland towns. The guidelines for the Structure Plan abstracted by the county planners from the exercise tended to lean most towards 1, which so far as Honiton was concerned implied a population of 12,000 by 2001. The guidelines did stress the desirability of locating additional employment opportunities at Honiton. Of a number of statutory authorities who were asked to comment on the three published options, only the Water Authority made comments relevant to the Honiton area. From their point of view, Option 1, with its emphasis on linked but relatively remote settlements, made the best immediate use of existing investment. Concentration on Exeter and the coast could risk coastal pollution while emphasis on inland towns, including Honiton, could lead to difficulties over effluent standards where sewage was being discharged into small inland streams.

These discussions entered into the calculations which now formed part of the *Report of Survey*, published in 1977 for the Structure Plan. Inevitably the *Report* had to venture into the difficult field of population trends, for, as the County Planning Officer pointed out in a paper submitted to the Structure Plan sub-committee, 'the question of population change over the Structure Plan period to 1991 is basic to the formulation of the strategic policies which will emerge'. For population projections, national demographic factors such as changes in the fertility rate had to be assessed in relation to migration levels, and these were different, both in extent and in age composition, according to which past five-year period was analysed. 1961 and 1971 were census years, and there had been a 10 per cent sample census in 1966. 1976 was an estimate. Assuming that the 1966 and 1976 figures were not misleading, the data suggested three different levels of migration, the latest being the highest.

The date to which the report looked forward was 1991, ten years earlier than the 'target' date for the SWEPC study or the Exeter sub-regional study, and 20 years earlier than the date to which the 1969 *Exeter and District Joint Feasibility Study* had addressed itself. The population figures are therefore not comparable, quite apart from differences due to new evidence of change. For the Exeter and East Devon area, the likely maximum influx was put at 62,000, i.e. a 21 per cent increase (a figure which EDDC seems to have thought replaced the 77,000 of the Sub-Regional Study, though this of course was a projection to 2001). If the lowest assumptions were fulfilled, the increase could be as low as 32,000.

The *Report of Survey* concluded that the pressures for development continued, broadly speaking, to affect the south and east, especially the coasts and the Plymouth area, plus the Barnstaple/Bideford area of North Devon, but outside these areas rural depopulation[1] and declining services were the hall-mark. The great question was — could, and if so should, the process be reversed? The key inland towns were intended to provide focal points of economic and social life in the rural areas, but Honiton, it had to be admitted, was more or less within the ambit of the sub-regional centre, Exeter.

For the consultation stage of the Structure Plan[2] five options were put before the people of Devon:

1) to concentrate future development into five 'areas of major change' already possessing a wide range of facilities;

2) to accept the attraction of the main urban centres but endeavour to spread population and jobs more widely;

3) positively to encourage development in areas with less immediate potential;

4) to give priority to remote and declining, i.e. assisted areas;

5) to build up the coasts for tourism and retirement.

So far as Exeter and East Devon were concerned, the population increase to be expected and for whom a settlement pattern had to be devised was estimated at 49,700 to 65,600, varying according to the options chosen. In all options, Honiton retained the same status, that of an Area Centre (analogous to the former coastal and key inland towns). No population break-down by individual settlement was offered, but the land allocation suggested in all five options was only ten acres above that in Honiton's extant outline development plan, which had envisaged a 1991 population of 10,000. East Devon District Council did not commit their support to any option, but the general tenor of their response was to support proposals that allowed for gradual expansion and the checking of rural depopulation. Therefore they opposed major expansion at Exeter, and disapproved of rigidly defined hierarchies of villages to which blanket proposals were supposed to apply, preferring to leave flexibility with the district councils who might be expected to know more about the individual circumstances of different settlements. They welcomed any proposal to help Honiton develop as an independent centre.

Fifteen months after the publication of the *Report of Survey*, the *Draft Written Statement* for the Structure Plan was published. In that relatively short space of time, the expectations about population change had undergone such extensive revision that the Exeter/East Devon area, subject in SWEPC's 1975 forecast to an increase of 90,000 by 2001, had diminished via the 30,000–to–62,000–by–1991 of the *Report of Survey*,

---

[1]The 1981 census was to reveal that the tide of population movement had in fact reversed, and was moving into rural areas, both the remote and the less remote.

[2]*Structure Plan Phase IV. The Structural Options and Draft Policies/Proposals.*

and the 49,700–to–65,000 of the *The Structural Options*, to a new assessment of 25,000 to 36,000 in the *Draft Written Statement*. So far as Honiton was concerned, the allocations reverted to the outline development plan allocation for 10,000 in 1991. And this was the assessment which appeared in the final *Structure Plan*, approved by Devon County Council in November 1979, and finally accepted by the Secretary of State in April 1981.

V

LAND ALLOCATION AND INFRASTRUCTURE

The vehicle by which the long term assumptions of county planning are translated into the specific land-use provisions on which development control decisions are based has, throughout the period under review, been the outline development plan. These local, non-statutory instruments developed *ad hoc* in the late 1950s and early 1960s, with ministerial cognisance of such instruments dating from a reference, in *Planning Bulletin No. 1* of 1962, to the value of 'informal town centre maps'. Their precise status was at first rather a puzzle. In April 1966 Honiton Municipal Borough Council, then debating a draft outline development plan prepared by the County, enquired of the County whether they should be disclosed to solicitors making 'searches', but were told that 'in the absence of any specific request for details in connection with the Outline Plan, there would appear to be no necessity to discuss its existence. If any information is given, it should be made clear that the Outline Plan is a plan merely for the guidance of the local planning authority in dealing with development applications.' But by July 1966 the County's view had changed and they were pressing the suggestion that outline development plans should be advertised to local people. Their significance was acknowledged in 1967 when *Planning Bulletin No. 8,* having extended recognition of informal plans from town centres to 'small towns and villages', remarked that the Minister would 'have regard to' these plans in adjudicating on planning appeals. This settled the point, which Honiton's Town Clerk was raising at about that time, that the attempt to 'bind' the County, the Borough and the public at large by 'a flourish of maps and written statements' seemed to be 'a collossal bluff' since it had no sanction in any Town or Country Planning Act.

Agreeing an ODP for Honiton proved a difficult and tedious business. The first draft prepared by the County was presented to the Borough in March 1965, and was not well received, partly for a number of minor reasons to which over the course of time solutions were found, but also for one reason of substance, the Borough's objection to the proposed limit on the size of Honiton as indicated by the 'urban fence', or boundary beyond which development was not to be permitted. The Borough wanted to extend the town limits much further, to the edge of the Area of Outstanding Natural Beauty south of the town (see Figures 3 and 4). The County pointed out that this would have extended develop-able land from 80 acres (to accommodate 2,000 people) to 438 acres, an extension to which there were agricultural and amenity objections.

The Borough's constant attempts to find words to incorporate in the plan which would enable them to leap the urban fence (e.g. their suggestion of the phrase 'the Authority will not normally permit new houses or other development in areas outside the town except on the merits of a particular case') met with equally constant rejection from the County, until, in the summer of 1966, rumours reached the Borough of the overspill recommendations for their area. Assured by the County that this would indeed lead to the re-opening of the whole question of projected size when the second review of the County Development Plan was undertaken, the Borough decided to postpone agreeing the Plan. The County continued to ply them with new forms of words but when, in 1967, discussions took place about the proposed feasibility study for siting 20,000 people in the area, the Borough felt it had a perfect excuse for again refusing to agree the plan. None of these manoeuvres appear to have been of any practical significance, since the County were the local planning authority, so the unsigned plan remained the basis for the County's development control decisions.

This was a period of exceptionally rapid development. Allocated land was being absorbed so rapidly that by early 1968 it was evident that at current rates only six years supply of land remained of what was intended to provide for expected population up to 1981. Further land was needed without awaiting the outcome of the feasibility study, and the County proposed an amendment to the unagreed plan, giving a revised 1981 population projection and adding a further 60 acres to the land open for development. Unfortunately, the plan now submitted for the Borough's agreement was the original 1965 plan (plus the 60 acre amendment), lacking all the minor amendments which had been so painstakingly achieved. It was a small administrative error, but in the prevailing climate it was enough to precipitate another firm rejection of the plan by the Borough, who took the opportunity to re-open the whole issue of the limitations on the town's size. The 1965 draft, the one so unfortunately again presented to the Borough, had used the phrase 'the Authority will not normally permit new houses or other development in those areas outside the town unless, on the merits of the particular case, there is acceptable agricultural need as provided in the Development Plan'. The County had in early 1967 agreed to amend this to read 'the Outline Development Plan does not affect the policy of the Local Planning Authority when dealing with applications for development in the Countryside'. The accidental reversion to the earlier phraseology moved the Clerk to point out that the phrase was a repetition of one in the *County Development Plan* referring to limits to development in rural areas round villages. Honiton was no village, but a key inland town where, in the words of the County Plan, 'industrial and residential development should be encouraged'.

The Honiton ODP, with a freshly amended population projection for 1981 of 6,350, was finally adopted by both Councils in the autumn of 1969, all interest having long since switched to the far more ambitious feasibility study in which, incidentally, the 'landscape and amenity' considerations which had played so big a part in the controversy about the urban fence had disappeared from the analysis on potential limits to growth. With the County's promise to embark on a wholly new ODP, the adoption was seen as an interim measure. With hindsight it is possible to say, incidentally, that the 1969 population projection for 1981 was to prove almost correct, subsequent upward revisions proving to be overestimates.

As Appendix 4 shows, the hectic pace of housebuilding in the late Sixties was not to be maintained, but at the time, with almost annual upward revisions of the population forecasts, sewerage looked like being a problem. Prior to the 1974 reorganisation which gave responsibility to the Water Authorities, Honiton Borough Council, ever-aware of their expansionist ambitions, had undertaken considerable expenditure. Devon County Council had in 1965 approved a grant of nearly £2,000 per annum towards reconstruction costs estimated at £82,500, an estimate which later escalated through inflation to £95,462 and attracted a £30,600 lump sum contribution from the County. There were surface drainage problems, the effluent into the River Otter was below standard and the filters, for special local reasons, overloaded; but remedial work was expected to ensure that the works would function to a design capacity of 6,500 people, which in 1968, when the consultants' report on the works was made, would not have been reached for many years, for current population including the Army was reckoned at not much above 5,000 and the outline development plan agreed in 1969 had provided for a smaller population than that (6,350) by 1981. The feasibility study on Honiton in 1968 looked closely at the water supply and sewage disposal facilities, and concluded that so far as water was concerned, adequate supplies would probably be available for normal growth up to about 1981, after which extra could be obtained for a total population of up to 10,000 from supplies at Ottery St Mary, but this would require reinforcement of three or four miles of mains. So far as sewerage was concerned, the feasibility study advised that if some £135,000 were spent on improving the existing system, future expansion would be possible by adding units capable of servicing 5,000 until a total population of 20,000 was reached — after which another site would have to be found and a new sewage works built.

The feasibility study of 1968 had suggested that even without a town development scheme, population might well reach 8,000 by 1981, requiring, according to the study, a further 167 acres of land to be

31

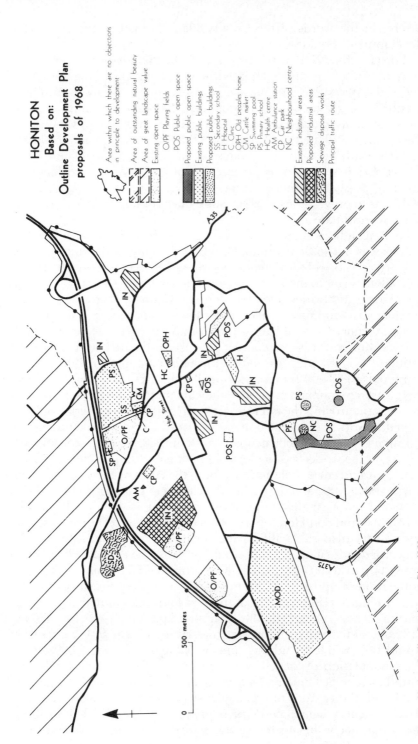

HONITON
Based on:
Outline Development Plan
proposals of 1968

Area within which there are no objections
in principle to development

Area of outstanding natural beauty

Area of great landscape value

Existing open space

O/PF Playing fields

POS Public open space

Proposed public open space

Existing public buildings

Proposed public buildings
SS Secondary school
H Hospital
C Clinic
OPH Old peoples home
CM Cattle market
SP Swimming pool
PS Primary school
HC Health centre
AM Ambulance station
CP Car park
NC Neighbourhood centre

Existing industrial areas

Proposed industrial areas

Sewage disposal works

Principal traffic route

Fig. 3   Honiton Outline Development Plan 1968

32

allocated for development. The concluding words of the study were

> the assessment of future growth and the identification of a major area
> suitable for this south of the existing town and centred between the trunk
> road towards Axminister (A35) and the Sidmouth Road (A375) in this
> study[1] . . . should be major considerations in framing further policies to
> guide the development of Honiton, whether or not a minimum town
> development scheme is attempted. The Local Planning Authority's outline
> plan for the borough should reflect these, with appropriate programme
> provisions.

Without waiting for any revision of the ODP, the Borough Council in
mid-1969 had approached the Ministry of Housing and Local Government to ascertain whether they would sanction preliminary work
towards an extension of the works to cope with 10,000. The Ministry
agreed, 'provided the forecast of population increase can be justified',
which the Borough Council felt had been amply done in the Honiton
and Exeter feasibility studies. The Ministry accordingly agreed to
tenders being sought. However, the advice from consultants persuaded
the Borough that various problems involved in the suggested
improvements made it more economical to revise the entire scheme,
and plan for a population of 12,000. Approval for a first phase was
obtained from the Ministry, Devon County agreed to give grant aid,
and in April 1972 the Borough applied for loan sanction for some
£500,000. Meanwhile, effluent standards had become so bad that in
1972 an embargo on development was imposed, and it was agreed to
make local improvements that would raise effluent standards
sufficiently to cover a population of 7,300. During 1971 a tender of
£32,000 plus was accepted. It was hoped that the major work would be
complete by March 1974, and the embargo was in fact raised in 1973.

In 1970 planning applications were coming in for residential building
beyond the area agreed in the outline plan, and were turned down by the
Borough on the grounds that they would overload the works, which
were then undergoing remedial work on effluent standards. In an echo
of the long-running controversy between Borough and County about
building outside the 'urban fence', the County insisted that while it was
true the works would be overloaded, the stress should be on the fact that
the proposed development was 'outside the area within which there is
no fundamental objection to development'. The Borough produced a
composite and not wholly logical wording, saying that most of the land
concerned was 'at present outside the Honiton outline plan area' and
development would 'therefore' be 'premature' because it would
overload the existing sewerage system.

In December 1970 a circular was issued by the Department of the
Environment (*Land Availability for Housing*, Circular 10/70) calling on

[1]See Figure 3.

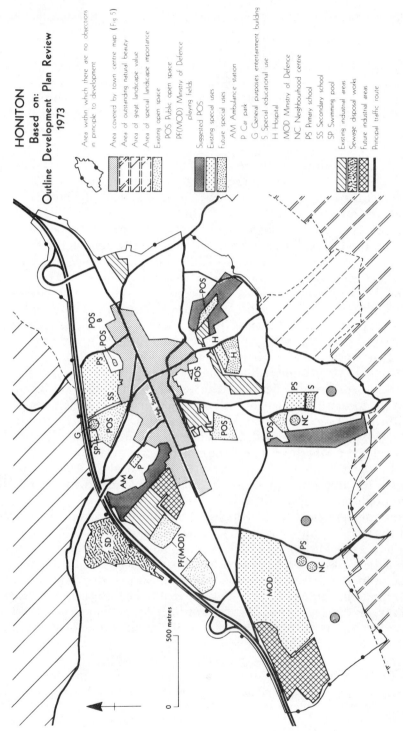

HONITON
Based on:
Outline Development Plan Review
1973

Area within which there are no objections in principle to development

Area covered by town centre map (Fig 5)

Area of outstanding natural beauty

Area of great landscape value

Area of special landscape importance

Existing open space

POS Public open space

PF(MOD) Ministry of Defence playing fields

Suggested POS

Existing special uses

Future special uses

AM Ambulance station

P Car park

G General purposes entertainment building

S Special educational use

H Hospital

MOD Ministry of Defence

NC Neighbourhood centre

PS Primary school

SS Secondary school

SP Swimming pool

Existing industrial areas

Sewage disposal works

Future industrial areas

Principal traffic route

500 metres

Fig. 4 Honiton Outline Development Plan 1974

34

Courtesy Ministry of Defence

Honiton aerial view

local authorities to do all they could to facilitate the release of land for housing since 'the availability of land for development is essential to the stability of land prices and to the revival of the house-building programme'; a statement which bore indirect witness to the concern being felt at the time over the very rapid inflation then affecting the price of building land. The County Planning Officer's March 1971 report on land availability for housing, prepared in response to this circular, included Honiton as one town where more land was likely to be made available as a result of the current outline plan review.

The *Honiton Report*, which formed the basis of the revised ouline development plan and which included a town centre study, was published in 1973 and, with minor amendments, agreed by both authorities early in 1974. It looked forward to 1991 and selected a population figure of 10,000. It found that 110 of the acres allocated for development in 1969 remained undeveloped, including enough residential land to house about 2,350 people at 10 dwellings to the acre with 2.6 per dwelling, or 26 per acre. This was a considerable reduction in assumptions about occupancy levels, for the original 1965 assessment had allowed for 80 acres to house 2,000 people, or 40 people per acre, and the change was reflected in a considerable extension of the proposed acreage, adding a further 105 acres to the town area with potential for a further 1,950 people. These figures were rounded off to give a reading of 220 acres of residential land, and that or something close to it is used in all subsequent planning documents, and for Honiton's allocation in the Structure Plan.

One of the Borough's last resolutions before its disappearance as an authority responsible for sewerage was to request the new council to give priority to sewerage schemes affecting the development of the town.

In 1974 the South West Water Authority came into being, taking over ultimate responsibility for both water and sewage. A note by Devon County's corporate management team later that year comments that in 1972 over 65 per cent of the classified settlements in the old Devon County were subject to restriction, including nine of the 13 key inland towns; that the financial situation was worsening; and that schemes submitted to SWWA totalled £21.2 million, while SWWA had only £8.5 million available. By 1974 however only six of the 13 key inland towns were subject to restriction, and Honiton was not among them. The new sewage works had come into operation early in 1974, at which time part of the old works was demolished, thus reducing capacity below the 12,000 target previously intended. The new Water Authority assessed the capacity of the combined new and old works at 10,500. In October 1975 the SWWA sought the views of Devon County Council in drawing up a list of priority schemes, and Honiton figured in a not-very-urgent section as requiring attention since 'the sub-regional feasibility study implies the necessity of additional infrastructure to allow for implementation of the outline development plan' — this being, of course, by then, the revised ODP proposing 10,000 by 1991.

The land allocation allowed for only 10,000 people in 1991 and the sewage works had a capacity of 10,500, so all appeared to be well, but two other factors were taken into consideration by the Water Authority as a result of which the Structure Plan had to list Honiton as a town where extensions to the sewage treatment works would be required by 1986–88. Firstly, the Authority calculated that adjacent hamlets draining to the Honiton works and temporary visitors (tourists) would account for some 900 and 220 people respectively, an input not previously explicitly allowed for in the population statistics, but equivalent to some 10 per cent of the total capacity. They also assessed the camp, vacated by the Army in 1971 but later bought by the District Council for industrial use, as the equivalent of 400 houses, roughly another thousand people assuming an average occupancy level of about 2.65, though obviously this was a notional figure, since much would depend on the precise type of industry and the sort of strain its effluent would put on the sewage treatment works. These two elements meant that, if the allocated building land was taken up, the stage at which sewerage extensions were needed would be reached before 1991.

In March 1980 the Water Authority had to ask for a temporary embargo on planning consents, due to difficulties over water supply. Remedial measures re-instated the supply, but probably at the cost of a diminished priority for a major water supply scheme — thus enhancing the likelihood of further problems in future. By March 1981 the supply embargo had ended, but there was concern over water quality, and sewerage commitments had reached a stage which, if implemented, would absorb all remaining capacity. A complete embargo on further development permissions had to be imposed.[1]

Since the present population is only 6,500 and the works have a capacity for 10,500, the situation appears, on the face of it, somewhat quizzical. There are, indeed, deep disagreements between the Water Authority and the District Council as to the necessity for the embargo; disagreements whose origin lies in the notional demand postulated for such unknown variables as the impact of summer tourism or the possibility of effluent-generating activities on the industrial estate, not to mention some variation in the assumptions made about occupancy levels. Similar problems elsewhere in the late 1970s prompted East Devon District Council to support the Devon Branch of the Association

[1]The Water Authorities cannot impose an 'embargo' on development, but local authorities respect requests from the Water Authorities to withold planning permission where facilities are inadequate, and in these circumstances the Secretary of State has not acceded to appeals by would-be developers. Should a local authority in these circumstances give planning permission, it would be open to the Water Authority to ask the Secretary of State to revoke permission.

of District Councils in its plea that responsibility for sewerage should be transferred to district councils, and that there should be increased representation of district councils on regional water authorities. In July 1982, however, following publication earlier in the year of a consultative paper on the subject[1], the Government, in the teeth of considerable opposition especially from local authorities, announced its intention to introduce a bill altering the structure of Water Authorities in the contrary direction. The proposals will not only reduce the total numbers serving on the Water Boards but will also make *all* members, instead of the present minority, direct appointees of the Secretary of State for the Environment; though this does not exclude the possibility of some appointees being from local authorities.

In practice, the South West Water Authority, in assessing what priorities to give to the various problems all over the area, formulates its policy in close liaison with the several counties involved. The simple explanation of the inadequacies encountered is shortage of resources. At one time there was doubt whether even the cost of fully commissioning the existing Honiton facilities could be met, and references abound to the 'stringent controls on public spending'.

Prior to the 1973 oil crisis, and even for a year or two after it, planning documents are remarkably cavalier on the subject of resource availability. The original AIC report of 1966, the progenitor of so many feasibility studies, had based its case for planned population increases in Devon partly on the assertion that only thus could Devon tap national government resources for the provision of infrastructure. It had taken for granted that those resources would be available. SWEPC's 1967 *Region with a Future* rather airily dismissed the matter with the remark 'the Council have not had to budget for a costed and dated programme, nor is the information available at this time for such an exercise', adding confidently 'it is fair to say that the Council have been reasonably optimistic about the rate of growth to be expected of the national economy'. These words were published just before the 1967 sterling crisis destroyed all prospect of Labour's National Plan achieving its objectives. The 1969 second review of the *County Development Plan* did not explore the subject. SWEPC's *Strategic Settlement Pattern* of 1974 returned to the subject, but in as bland a fashion as before, remarking only 'we think it reasonable to expect that the Government will ensure that national investment resources will be forthcoming to realise the policies of approved structure plans based on this strategic settlement pattern'.

The Town and Country Planning Act of 1971 under which structure plans are prepared requires that 'regard should be had to the resources

[1] *The Membership of Regional Water Authorities*, Department of the Environment Consultation Paper, January, 1982.

likely to be available in the structure plan period'. The new Devon County Council which came into being in April 1974 was already under the shadow of the economic dislocations following the first oil crisis. They had no hesitation in declaring, of SWEPC's recently published population forecasts, that they could not afford the extent of change envisaged. A greater proportion of the burden must fall on national rather than local resources. The Council's first response to SWEPC's *Strategic Settlement Pattern* was to resolve that the

> growth envisaged by the strategic report will impose very heavy burdens on the County Council's already overstretched resources and those of voluntary bodies, and the County Council will therefore require assurances of considerable financial support from central government over a prolonged period of years to meet the increased demands for community facilities like education, transportation, water and sewerage, social services and leisure facilities etc. The present infrastructure is not adequate for the existing population, and has failed to keep pace over the 30 years with the changes in population movement and the attitude to pollution. . . .

The Minister, however, in accepting SWEPC's proposals in August 1975 cautioned that

> the requirements for overcoming present deficiencies and meeting future needs will be identified in the region's Structure Plans, though claims for Government financial support for the required increases in investment and services will need to be carefully considered within the context of available national resources.

The new Devon County Council had already been sharply confronted by the constraints imposed by shortage of investment resources. Early in the life of the new Council the chief officers reported to the Council that development was being delayed because land was in many ownerships. There was a problem of 'unlocking' development land, and the solution was for local authorities to acquire large blocks of land, put in the roads and services and then make the land available for private and council housing, at the same time allocating appropriate sites for schools etc. The old Devon County Council had approved such a policy (which had indeed been canvassed in the Honiton feasibility study, in connection with a town development scheme), and the officers reported that Honiton was one of the areas where land suitable for local authority purchase had been identified.

An ambitious programme, to be funded by means of a 'roll-up' loan from merchant bankers, who would recoup when the improved land was sold, had been in course of negotiation, but the 'changed economic climate' had made such a scheme prohibitively expensive. The spanner thrust in the works of the western economies by the Yom Kippur war and the economic dislocation engendered by the resultant oil crisis was taking its toll. Nor was land the only commodity for which funds could not be found. In February 1976 the County Engineer reported

> There are many examples emerging where housing and industrial development is proposed by a private developer or district council which is subject to deferment because the proposal would necessitate expenditure on highways by the County Council . . . . It is clear that the programmes for housebuilding and industrial development are not subject to such a severe cut-back as highway expenditure, and whereas in the past it was possible to keep proposals in phase, this is no longer the case.

The County Engineer went on to describe the various criteria by which highways schemes were assessed for priority (accidents, traffic delays etc.) pointing out that new development did not automatically warrant top priority. He suggested that site developers should be asked to provide a contribution to highway construction essential to their developments. By 1976 the Devon Conservation Forum[1] published a paper, *Urbanisation in Devon*, including the comment

> We were told of many towns and villages where the provision of schools, social service centres, libraries, sewage works, road works, had fallen behind the growth of population. . . . Devon is unable to meet the needs of its existing population, as is made clear by the inadequacy of public investment in the county, the shortages of school and hospital places, the sewerage embargoes and the housing problems. . . .

The 1977 *Report of Survey* for the Structure Plan explained the South West Water Authority's programme for 1975/76 to 1980/81, but 'as an indication of the considerable task which confronts the Water Authority in seeking to assist with the infrastructure', it also printed a table showing that 50 per cent of the 'classified' settlements in the 1969 *County Development Plan* were subject to restrictions on development because of water or sewerage inadequacies. The final Structure Plan quoted the SWWA's hope that the level of investment required could be accommodated if suitably phased within future capital programmes, but with the proviso that this was dependent on 'overall capital expenditure being maintained at current levels and no greater expenditure being incurred than at present on the renewal of existing assets' plus various other contingencies which could change their assumptions.

The *Report of Survey* in 1977 included an account of national government proposals on public expenditure, showing that for the four years 1976–1980 the (then Labour) Government intended progressive reductions each year in local authority capital expenditure under every

---

[1] The Forum arose out of European Conservation Year 1970, and was established on County Council initiative as a standing liaison committee of the major bodies concerned with the County's environment. It held its first meeting in 1972.

heading, though with a small upturn at the end of the period for housing and for health and social services. The *Report* commented 'Capital expenditure will, by the year 1979/80, be very much reduced if present trends continue. Furthermore, it must be assumed that during the period up to 1991, the situation will not radically alter.'

The *Draft Written Statement* had a later White Paper on public expenditure on which to draw for guidance, which showed many changes of detail with annual increases between 1978 and 1982, but nevertheless during the first six years of the structure plan period there would be 'severe restrictions in the levels of public expenditure', with the 1981/82 level still 14 per cent below that for 1976/77. This assessment still stood at the time of publication of the final Structure Plan in 1979. After the 1979 general election, the new administration's first White Paper on Expenditure (Cmnd 7746) began with the words 'Over the years public spending has been increased on assumptions about economic growth which have not been achieved.' Rejecting the alternatives of increased taxation or deficit spending, the new Government declared its intention to lower the planned levels of local authority capital expenditure in 1980/81 to some eight per cent below the planned 1979/1980 figure. The following year's White Paper on Expenditure (Cmnd 8175 of March 1981) proceeded on the new policy of cash limits with the allocation of priorities left to local decision, but the limits envisaged a further decline of three per cent in 1982/83 and of four per cent in 1982/84.

The assumptions about economic growth have offered lamentably poor guidance. The National Plan of 1965 had posited an annual growth rate of nearly four per cent over the six years 1964–1970. Only 2.4 per cent had been achieved, and long before six years were up, the plan had been interred. 'Plan' was a description that dropped out of use, being replaced by more hypothetical words such as 'assessment' or 'scenario'. The Treasury's 'Scenario II' target for growth in manufacturing industry from 1971 to 1975 was 7.9 per cent per annum, but the actual achievement, following the oil crisis, miners' strike and three-day week, averaged 0.4 per cent. Undeterred, the Government in 1976 presented to the National Economic Development Council a new Scenario II involving a growth rate in manufacturing industry of 7.9 per cent per annum from 1975 to 1979. By 1978 the rate actually achieved was 0.7 per cent. Since then there has been either no growth at all or actual decline.

In Honiton at present the Water Authority have not the resources to service the new residential land, and even some of the extant planning permissions have only been made possible because a major developer is prepared to install a pumping station to enable the development to drain to the sewage works. If the cost passes to the purchasers of the new houses, this will at least have the merit of ensuring that new

41

installations are paid for by those who make them necessary. But although there were, in 1980, permissions extant to five substantial construction companies totalling between 700 and 800 houses, in fact in 1981 only 13 new private houses were completed (see Appendix 4). Of 144 jobs lost in 1980 from 186 firms in Honiton, 90 were from firms associated with the building trades.[1] The virtual cessation of building was thus certainly not due to the embargo on new planning permissions. It was due in all probability to a lack of demand, probably resulting from the high interest rates which immobilised the housing market by frightening would-be movers off the risk of having to obtain bridging loans.

Thus the economic stagnation which atrophied the provision of new sewerage also atrophied the need for it, both being symptoms of national economic difficulties. Yet it was precisely to stimulate economic growth that so much of the planning of the Sixties and Seventies was concerned. The next chapter looks at the efforts made to achieve in Honiton investment for purposes of economic prosperity, and of how employment and business enterprise have fared over the two decades.

[1]A. Glyn-Jones, *Small Firms in a Country Town* (University of Exeter and Devon County Council, 1982).

VI

THE LOCAL ECONOMY

Two themes with regard to the economy alternate in the discussions and documents of the Sixties and Seventies. From the AIC report of 1965 to the SWEPC *Strategic Settlement Pattern* of 1974, the emphasis is on economic growth for its own sake. AIC had stressed the need to seek out and employ women who were not registering for work, and had shown some antipathy towards the suspected dilatoriness of part-timers and the self-employed. As the Sixties wore on, controversy developed over the goal of economic growth, as measured by GNP statistics nourished by but limited to any and every form of financially-measurable expenditure; and doubts began to be raised as to whether the price, in terms of pollution or of destruction of the natural environment for instance, might not be too high. The last half of the Sixties saw the emergence in Britain of organisations like Friends of the Earth and the Conservation Society, stressing such concepts as quality of life. SWEPC's 1974 report side-stepped the dilemma without equivocation. 'The quality of life in the South West' it stated 'depends on sustained economic growth.' 'There are parts of the region with great potential for economic growth which are well placed to benefit from the high level of national economic activity which is the objective of all UK governments.' Wages, pointed out SWEPC, were lower in the South West than the average for Great Britain. The problem for the future was to create an upward pressure on wages by ensuring that jobs were provided faster than labour became available[1] — no small task, for, as the report noted, 'Efforts to stimulate employment growth for the purpose of raising the demand for labour will be offset by the incentive thus provided for working people to move into the region and so tend to reduce the pressure of demand to its former level.' Confidence that this could be achieved ebbed rather than flowed over succeeding years, and by the time the *Report of Survey* for the Structure Plan was published in 1977 the pessimistic probability was being suggested that the larger the number of people of working age who moved into Devon actively seeking work, the higher the level of unemployment was likely to be. Perhaps, this section of the *Report* forlornly concluded, some oil would

---

[1] The Devon Conservation Forum's publication *Urbanisation in Devon* (1976) was suspicious of this motive for attracting industry, maintaining that most of Britain was 'sub-average' compared with the affluent South East, and that the main Devon low-wage sector was agriculture, which could only be helped by negotiations at national level.

be found off the coast of the South West? Or perhaps there would be 'new types of service sector industries'? But 'there is little sign of such development at the present time'.

Unemployment, rather than economic expansion for its own sake, had been the dominant concern of economic aspirations in the late Fifties and early Sixties in Devon, and became so again at the end of the Seventies. In both periods, youth unemployment was of particular concern; not so much, in the earlier period, because of *actual* youth unemployment as because lack of opportunity was held to account for the tendency of the young to migrate out of the County. The other side of the unemployment coin was the above-mentioned anxiety over the numbers of working age people moving in to the County, but the truth may be less contradictory than this paradox would suggest. It seems probable that the under-25s, for a variety of social, vocational, and not necessarily deleterious reasons, are attracted to cities; but that for older age groups cities cease to be so seductive.[1] Thus, SWEPC held that 'the essential objective of regional strategic planning in the South West must be to secure economic growth to match the population growth which is bound to occur'. When it came down to brass tacks, however, these worthy exhortations petered out into the rather vague assertion, so far as Economic Planning Area 14 covering Exeter and East Devon (including Honiton) was concerned, that 'there is scope for industrial development at some of the smaller centres in the area . . .'.

There is very little mention of actual, as distinct from potential unemployment in the Honiton area in the minutes of either Devon County Council or the Honiton Municipal Borough Council prior to local government reorganisation in 1974. Interest in job provision is discussed in terms of producing an upward pressure on wages; of diminishing the attractions to young people of the metropolitan areas; or of providing for a projected trend in in-migration. During these years unemployment in the Honiton Employment Exchange Area was worsening relative to Devon as a whole or to the UK, the peak disparity coming in 1969 and 1970, shortly after the house-building crescendo of 1967–1968, but by the census year of 1971 the disparity, though still present, was diminishing (see Appendices 3 and 4). But the precise relationship of migration to unemployment is unclear, not least because the Honiton area to which the unemployment statistics refer covers some 20 settlements, including Sidmouth, and disaggregated figures are not available. Some guidance does emerge from the census figures. The numbers of working age people in Honiton at the 1961 and 1971 censuses reflect of course not merely the age composition of migrants, but also the possible changes in age structure of the indigenous

[1]Hatherleigh in West Devon provided a precise statistical illustration of this in the years after 1971, with continuing emigration of the under-25s, but with the largest incoming group of any 10-year cohort being those aged 26–35. See A. Glyn-Jones, *Rural Recovery: Has it Begun?* 1979.

44

population — the proportion of old age pensioners, for instance is increasing nationally. Excluding soldiers from the 1961 census (they were no longer present in 1971) the proportion of working age people fell from 55.2 per cent in 1961 to 54.5 per cent in 1971, but since the total population increased over the decade, these percentages conceal an actual increase of about 600 in those of working age, (see Appendix 2). The economically active below the age of 65, according to the 10 per cent sample of the 1961 census, numbered about 1,830. By 1971 the economically active below pensionable age numbered about 2,075. Thus the increase of about 600 in those of working age resulted in an increase of about 250 in those seeking work, and most of them found it — there were only about 30 unemployed in 1961 (20 men and 10 women) and 64 in 1971 (46 men and 18 women). Nearly all the men under 65 (1,350 out of 1,460 approximately) were economically active in 1971, but not much more than half the women were (725 out of 1,375 approximately).

Planning applications during these years reveal that a process of modest small-scale change was afoot. Change-of-use permissions were sought for small private houses to be used for such purposes as antique shops, showrooms, a photographic studio, craft manufacture (granted provided 'no machinery be installed except electric sewing machines') or a haulage depot with not more than three lorries. Conditions placed on a small engineering firm proposing to come to a partially residential area were sufficiently stringent to deter the firm from coming (it remained in Sidmouth) but the main impediment to these modest developments came from Ministry of Transport objections to access arrangments, a topic which continues to rankle among the business community in Honiton. There were also delays caused by the requirement that land belonging to a statutory authority could not, by law, be offered to a private buyer until it had first been offered to, and rejected by, all other statutory authorities. A yard belonging to, but not wanted by, British Rail, and ardently desired by a developing merchant, was thus sterilised for a considerable period.

A study[1] of the development of industry and commerce in Honiton over this period suggests an increase from about 166 to 213 in the number of businesses operating (see Appendix 5). This covers the period in which the Honiton bypass opened, and it is evident that the shops did not suffer, though a transport café closed. A decline in the hotels and catering sector which occurred later is due largely to pub closures which probably resulted from the departure of the Army; simultaneously there was an upmarket drift with licensed restaurants replacing cafés. Since this was a period of house-building, the construction industry prospered, with an increase from 18 to 29 in local

[1]A. Glyn-Jones *Small Firms in a Country Town* (University of Exeter and Devon County Council, 1982).

High Street, Honiton

firms advertising as plumbers, painters and decorators, carpenters and joiners and electrical contractors. There were associated increases: firms of estate agents and surveyors increased from three to six, architects entered the list, and by 1971 two contractors' plant hire companies were operating. The increasing local population was reflected in an increase in hairdressing establishments, and in distribution and repairs, the main growth areas being in specialities like antiques, arts and crafts, jewellery, clothing and activities connected with selling and servicing motor cars. There is an increase in coach hire and road haulage operations, and the opening of a travel agency. Activities ancillary to business such as law and accountancy firms were also increasing. Manufacturing firms increased from 16 to 21, though one of the new firms failed to establish itself, and soon closed.

Throughout the Sixties, planning documents are permeated by a distrust of service industry employment and a hankering for manufacturing industry. The significance of service industry was not denied — indeed, the *Exeter and District Joint Feasibility Study* of 1969 pointed out that the large population increase foreseen was attributed to 'the migration to the area of retired people, the concentration and growth of institutional population in Exeter, and the consequent growth of service industries'. (The 'institutional' growth was envisaged as the expansion of the University, the centralisation and expansion of hospital facilities, and 'similar institutional expansion'.) The study further envisaged that 'a concentration of new office employment at Exeter could also engender growth', and added that 'the growth in office accomodation in Exeter has largely been achieved without help from the Location of Offices Bureau'.

The AIC report differed in emphasis from others only in the strength of its insistence that prosperity and employment needed to be based on a manufacturing proportion at least approaching the national average. The assumption was that this would not develop indigenously but must be imported, and to that there remained the two great impediments of Board of Trade decisions on the issue of Industrial Development Certificates, and the disadvantages of not being an assisted area. It was to overcome these difficulties that the search for a town development scheme had been undertaken. The *Exeter and District Joint Feasibility Study*, completed in the knowledge that no such scheme appeared practicable, commented:

> Employment throughout the City and the rest of the Region is . . . heavily dependent on service industry except at Tiverton and the study underlines the difficulty of introducing new manufacturing industry into the area under the present system of control of the location of industry otherwise than by means of a Government approved development scheme. The position is likely to be further exacerbated by the creation of an Intermediate Area around Plymouth.

The Hunt Committee on Intermediate Areas was then due to report, and the Joint Committee for the South West (the original sponsors of the first AIC report) lobbied the Committee to recommend that IDC's outside development areas should cease to be necessary for factories in the 5,000 to 10,000 square foot range. The Hunt Committee did so recommend, but the then Labour Government rejected the recommendation.[1]

It was not only a matter of *permitting* industry, it was a question of *attracting* it. As the Exeter study wistfully remarked at a time when the outcome of the Hunt deliberations was still not known, 'Despite the possibility of the Government relaxing its industrial location policies, it is unlikely that any substantial expansion of the manufacturing industry in the Region could take place without the adoption of a town development scheme which would ally the aid of the Government in attracting industry.'

There remained only such efforts as the local authorities could themselves afford. Honiton Municipal Borough Council had no power to buy land, or make loans, having missed the opportunity of which neighbouring districts had availed themselves under the Devon County Council Act of 1961. By the late Sixties the Borough were regretting this, but learnt to their chagrin that the situation could only be remedied by Act of Parliament, which the County did not intend, and the Borough could not afford, to promote, even assuming parliamentary time were to be made available.

Attempts by the County to assist in the provision of serviced land did not escape the resource constraints which, as the previous chapter recounted, affected the provision of sewerage or roads. Midway through 1967 the Ministry of Housing and Local Government had issued a statement pointing out that

> outside development areas, the number of mortgage advances made to industrialists by local authorites has grown steadily, and taken with the expenditure of local authorities on buying and laying out land for industrial estates and building factories to let, now represents a considerable part of the loan sanction for all planning purposes. Since it is the Government's expressed policy to give priority to industrial development within the development areas, it will be necessary, as from the date of this letter, to restrict severely the issue of loan sanction for industrial development to local authorities outside development areas. Regard will be had to the existence of special needs in particular places outside development areas, including places where planned expansion and relocation is taking place . . .'.

The County's Finance Committee pursued the question, but reluctantly recorded towards the end of the year that 'there seems to be little prospect of obtaining any relaxation in the loan sanction policy of

[1] In 1970 the new Conservative Government raised the limit for most areas, including the South West, to 10,000 square feet, followed in 1972 by a further increase to 15,000 square feet, where it remained until in 1974 Labour reduced the limit to 10,000 square feet. Two years later, in 1976, the applicable limit was again raised to 15,000 square feet. On the Conservatives' return to power in 1979, all need for IDCs was abolished for factories of less than 50,000 square feet. In December 1981, the entire system of IDCs was suspended, the Minister remarking that since 1975 only 28 of 7,000 applications had been refused.

the Ministry of Housing and Local Government'. The truth was, though, that as the County Land Agent was reporting at the end of 1968, the supply of sites for manufacturing industry on the Council's industrial estates in any case exceeded demand (though the reverse was the case for service industries). What is not clear is whether the sites being offered were too big for the only sizes (i.e. below 5,000 square feet until 1970) of factories which escaped the need of an IDC.

Towards the end of the decade 1960–1970, Devon County Council's Industry and Tourism Committee claimed that work for 49 people (38 men and 11 women) had been provided in Honiton by industries which had been brought in or assisted to expand through the Committee's activities. This presumably refers to the two local firms which, as Chapter II noted, were able to expand by transferring to the County estate from their existing premises in or near Honiton. There were other tentative enquiries, but they came to nothing. When the whole project was first mooted in 1965 the Borough had been told that it would probably take three to five years to develop the site, but in fact it was not until 1975 that a third company arrived.

The new local authorities which came into being in April 1974 were immediately faced with the economic dislocations that followed the quadrupling of oil prices. For 1975 the average rate of unemployment in the UK was over four per cent, in Devon 5.9 per cent and in the Honiton area 6.4 per cent. Unemployment mounted both nationally and locally, with the Honiton rate escalating more rapidly than the national until 1977. Might the time be approaching when a case could be made out for East Devon as an area worthy of government assistance? Devon's Economy and Employment Committee began a record of 'black spots', areas of Devon where unemployment was worse than the Devon average, and over the following years the Honiton area hovered on the borderline, qualifying for or escaping 'black spot' classification in alternate reports.

July, August and September usually had higher numbers out of work, in spite of the tourist season, than the preceding and following months. In March 1977 the County instigated enquiries into reports that 'unemployed people who do not wish to seek employment are taking up residence in various parts of Devon'. The Department of Employment had made an investigation on this topic in 1971 in the Teignmouth area, examining the records of all those registered as unemployed at any time from 1 January to 19 May 1971 — not a very sensible period, perhaps, since it concluded before the weather would have attracted the beachcombing element. They found that a quarter of the men and a fifth of the women had no 'local employment history' — in other words 'they had moved into the area without a firm prospect of employment, and this had clearly contributed to the rise in local unemployment'. The County decided to ask the Employment Services

Agency to provide figures on one inland town, one seaside resort and one rural area in Devon showing, for the months of January and July 1978, how many people had been unemployed for up to 13 weeks, but had been resident in the area for *less* than 13 weeks, i.e. had moved in while unemployed. Honiton, Teignmouth and Bovey Tracey were the three places used for the investigation.

For Honiton the analysis was conducted in February and in July, the proportions being slightly higher in February (24.5 per cent) than in July (22.8 per cent). The County enquired anxiously of the Department of Employment whether anything could be done to discourage this drift, but were told that there was no provision whereby an unemployed person could be financially penalised specifically for moving to an area of high unemployment, though anyone who actually left a job in order to migrate might be disqualified from receiving unemployment benefit for up to six weeks. The County then switched their enquiries to the Department of Health and Social Security, with reference to the payment of social security benefits to those who move to areas of high unemployment. They learnt that if single or childless people moved, ostensibly to find work, to certain specified areas where work was indeed plentiful, then if after two weeks they had not obtained work they would be specially interviewed and benefit might be witheld. Obviously this could hardly hold good in areas of high unemployment. This left the Council members very dissatisfied, and they voiced to Devon MPs their hope that some tighter control would be implemented.

When the figures are analysed by age, the evidence for young drifters moving to the South-West Riviera is less strong. The July analysis was broken down by age, and of the 26 recently arrived claimants with 13 weeks unemployment behind them, ten — nine men and a woman — were over 55. That still leaves 16 (14 per cent of those unemployed for 13 weeks), but it was reported that the Employment Service area managers had gained the impression, during this 'special exercise', that a high proportion of those moving to Devon were in the upper age groups with ultimate retirement in the area (e.g. occupational pensioners) as the main motivation. There was 'no indication' of a significant number of young single people moving in, though Honiton did report some movement 'from the London area' of a few women accompanying husbands who had got work in Honiton.

The extent to which the registration of early-retired occupational pensioners indicates a genuine pressure for employment is impossible to assess, as is the implication of such pressure on the type of jobs being sought. The Honiton Employment Exchange Area covers Sidmouth, a well-known retirement town with a very large percentage of elderly people and the strong probability of an 'early retired' component. Until 1974 the figures for the Honiton and Sidmouth offices were not separately available, and even after 1974 the unemployment *rate* as discussed by the County Economy and Employment Committee was that for the two offices combined, though the actual numbers were available separately from 1975.[1] Appendix 6 shows the proportions registered as unemployed in the age groups under 20, 20–54, 55–59 and 60 plus for men, and 55 plus for women, during the years since 1974.

The results show that at the Honiton exchange during these years of population increase largely through migration, the proportion of unemployed men aged over 60 was seldom less than about a third of the total, with a further 10 to 20 per cent aged over 55. For Sidmouth the proportions are higher — up to a (perhaps freak?) 82 per cent aged over 55 in 1974.

The County's Economy and Employment Committee recognised during the 1970s that crude unemployment rates were not a very reliable guide to an area's needs. From 1975 they were scrutinising not just the rates but the absolute numbers and in particular the ages involved. The 'black spot' classification, based solely on the rate, was amended by analyses of males under 55 out of work for more than six months; and of female 'activity rates', i.e. employment as a percentage of those aged 15 to 60 at the 1971 census; and the results were expressed in relation to a county average of 100. This resulted in a totally changed picture of need. In the summer of 1976 the Honiton Employment Exchange Area (i.e. the combined offices) showed only 62 men under 55 who had been out of work for six months, against 147 aged over 55; among those with a shorter history of unemployment, 43 per cent were over 55. Thus, while the unemployment rate alone put the Honiton index at 122 against a Devon County average of 100, the amended assessment brought the index figure to 69, making Honiton appear not a black spot but a favoured area. The female activity rate, incidentally, was slightly below average, with Honiton area at 98. During succeeding years, as Honiton continued to register as a 'black spot' in terms of the rate, the so-called 'needs index' continued to register relative advantage, with Honiton down to 67 in 1978, though the number of long-term unemployed males over 55 was increasing — by their own choice, if the increase was due to the inward migration of occupational pensioners. This is a not-implausible hypothesis given that (see Appendix 2) in Honiton itself (which does not of course constitute the whole employment exchange area) the age group 44 to 59 (female) or 64 (male) increased by 9.4 per cent in the decade 1971–81, while in Great Britain as a whole this age group declined in numbers by 7.6 per cent.

In the light of these indications Devon County's Employment and Economy Committee decided in 1976 not to regard the areas served by the Honiton, Exeter–Sowton and Exeter Airport industrial estates as

[1] The rate cannot be disaggregated because the total employment figure to which the rate is related is derived from employers over the whole area.

priority areas. Attempts would continue to develop the existing estates, but new ones would not be proposed. It was not a conclusion which pleased the East Devon District Council. On the contrary, late in 1980, with employment in the Honiton area at 7.8 per cent, much where it was in 1976, they applied to be granted Intermediate Area status. The national equivalent had by then moved from 5.7 per cent in 1976 to 7.4 per cent in 1980. Other areas were in far worse straits than East Devon, and the request was swiftly dismissed by the Department of Trade.

The disbursement of selective aid by central Government out of revenues garnered from the nation as a whole is a natural incentive to the authorities in every area to emphasise their problems and deprivations. It is an attitude hardly conducive to national morale, but highly understandable, and one which puts a very honourable gloss on Devon's efforts to establish the true implications of its unemployment figures. Not only is there the high proportion of over-55s registering in retirement areas, there is also, in areas like Devon with large numbers of self-employed people in farming and tourism, the probability that the base on which the unemployment *rate* is assessed is a smaller proportion of the working population than is the case in areas of large-scale industry. The unemployment rate is not strictly comparable as a measure of misery from one part of the country to another. But if the unemployment statistics provided no grounds for the attraction of special aid, another avenue opened up when special help, in the form of 'advance factories', became available for disadvantaged rural areas from the Development Commission.

In order to assess priorities in the disbursement of this aid, the Development Commission requested detailed submissions providing it with statistical evidence on which to base its decisions. In 1976 the County submitted the first in a series of Action Plans to the Development Commission. Their purpose was principally to describe the economic and demographic background to Devon so far as this was relevant to the work of the Development Commission and establish a priority list of settlements for further assistance by the Commission. In pursuit of this objective, analyses were prepared explaining the policies propounded by the County in successive plans, relating the Development Commission's terms of reference to Devon's developmental needs, and setting out, with accompanying maps and tables, the population changes by age, area and type of work over the period since 1961, the data being based chiefly on the 1971 census results. There were analyses of the employment structure by type and status, and, of course, the unemployment rates, expressed both as a percentage and in the form of the newly-devised 'needs index'.

The maps incorporated in the submission indicated, by parish, a considerable area of the County where rural depopulation was taking place, and it was this, rather than unemployment, that was emphasised in the submission — naturally enough, since the Commission's terms of reference limit it to rural regeneration, and the unemployment was being registered in the urban, not the rural areas. Comparison of 1961 and 1971 census data reveals that over the ten years, and allowing for boundary changes which affect comparability, seven of the 14 civil parishes in the Axminster Rural District lost population, as did seven of Honiton Rural District's 22 parishes. The submission suggested two 3,000 square feet advance factories in Honiton on Devon County's still unfilled industrial estate, and two of 2,500 square feet in Axminster where industrial land had been allocated, though at the time it was in private ownership or owned by British Rail.

East Devon District Council enthusiastically supported the County's stance. In Honiton the local Labour Party in 1977 petitioned the District to appoint an industrial development officer and seek out measures 'to attract light industrial development' in view of the unemployment and depopulation of the area. COSIRA asked the District Council to select 'pockets of need' where population was declining or disadvantaged, with a view to initiating action. The District recommended eight parishes in the Honiton Rural District. The exercise appears slightly strained, since five of the parishes had gained population in the census decade, three had lost, there being a net gain of eight people overall. Over the two rural districts as a whole, the census showed considerable population gains in both — of about a thousand in Axminster RD and seven hundred in Honiton RD; and though the proportions under pensionable age declined in both districts compared with the over 65s (who had markedly increased) the same trend was occurring nationally (Appendix 2). Absolute numbers under 45 increased in Honiton RD, but in Axminster RD the overall increase was due to the presence of the elderly. The 1981 census was to reveal (see Appendix 2) that the old Honiton municipal borough and its surrounding rural district both increased their proportion of younger working age people (age group 16–44) by far more than the national average, and Axminster also showed an increase though lower than the national average. All three areas showed overall population increases ranging from Honiton's 28 per cent to Axminster RD's marginal 0.4 per cent compared with a slight decline in the national figure.

The Development Commission returned a dusty answer on Axminster and Honiton. 'Honiton' they said 'is reasonably prosperous'. As for the two 2,500 square feet factories in Axminster, whose construction had been proposed for 1978/79, this matter would be deferred, pending evidence of East Devon District Council's willingness and ability to demonstrate 'self-help'.

The opportunity to which this comment referred was the departure of the Army from its Honiton camp, which in the course of time became available for other uses. From the middle of the 1970s interest was beginning to switch at both district and county level from laments over restrictions on large-scale industry to positive encouragement of small-scale. With 75 per cent of Devon's population in areas of the south and east never accorded any special status, the County's Economy and Employment Committee minuted that 'it is not encouraging to local authorities to commit funds for industrial development when manufacturing industry is discouraged from coming'. The County Estates Surveyor had been seeking abroad for the industrial investment that was not forthcoming at home, and since early 1975 had been engaged in a heavy programme of attendance at 'investment seminars' organised by the UK Government in Germany in an effort to interest German firms. In May of that year he reported from Frankfurt, in November from Koblenz, the following year he was at Mannheim, Stuttgart and Kassell, and in 1977 at Bremen. But as the economic recession worsened internationally, it became increasingly obvious that footloose investment was in desperately short supply, and that serious attention must be given to much more modest endeavours.

During 1977 county council Minutes make a number of references to proposals for purpose-built, county-financed 'small industrial units', and investigations were begun into possibilities of partnership, whether with the Development Commission or with private developers, to build small workshops for letting in North Devon. At the end of 1977 the size of 'small' was evidenced when the County Estates Surveyor's report stated that demand existed in Barnstaple for three factories of 5,000 square feet, three of 2,500 square feet, and 10 of 1,000 square feet. For the smaller settlements he recommended a search for small industrial sites which could be quickly and economically developed, and which, because of their size, would have a relatively slight effect on the environment; and for former industrial or similar buildings which by re-furbishing could be made available at reasonably low rents. The County voted £100,000 in 1978 for land acquisition for these purposes, and discussed proposals for constructing 2,000 and 3,000 square feet units within blocks of 10,000 square feet.

The Chairman of East Devon District Council had during 1975 been lamenting the lack of information on sites that might be available in the District for setting up small businesses, members had agreed that there should be 'a policy of encouraging small businesses' and that it should be made known that anyone wishing to expand their business should make their needs known to the District Secretary. As soon as it was known that the Army camp was available, the District inspected it and began negotiations to acquire it. Conveyance to the District Council was completed in March 1978.

There were about 80 living-huts in the camp. The District found some of them already occupied by local entrepreneurs who had obtained temporary tenancy agreements from the Property Services

Devon County Council Industrial Estate   Andrew Teed

Agency. Within a few months of the District's purchase they had received '37 firm enquiries for premises and sites' at the camp, 'together with many other informal enquiries', and six months later a further 33 applications were recorded. The Minutes do not, in most cases, state what size premises were being sought, but of nine which do give an indication, seven state a size of under 800 square feet, refer to wanting 'garage or larger for one-man business' or mention 'two to three employees'. The rents for the huts, which were mostly in poor condition, were in the region of 25p to 50p per square foot, compared with the average in the locality of about £1.40 to £1.50. The low price and the poor conditions certainly found a market. It will not last, as the roads and most of the buildings are below statutory standards and are being replaced. To bring the roads up to a standard that will accept the largest commercial vehicles will involve destroying a number of the huts, and will necessitate, in order that each may have direct access, the creation of larger sites, nearly all of them a minimum of one acre (permitting covered areas of about 20,000 square feet).

There is a marked contrast between the speed with which the relatively poor quality camp premises built up employment, and that on the more ambitious county industrial estate. At the camp, within three years of its becoming available, 23 firms were at work employing

296 people. At the industrial estate, thirteen years after its inception, five firms were at work employing 218 people. Expectations had perhaps always tended to be unrealistic, with the old Borough Council holding out for substantial migrant employers, opposing the relocation to the estate of existing local businesses, though they later modified this to a willingness to encourage industry, local or not, provided it employed 20 or more people. Devon County Council shared these aspirations for the first ten years of the estate's existence, but by 1977 the resolve to find labour-intensive manufacturing industry weakened, and land was leased for a brewery distribution depot. It does not follow, however, that had the County built an estate of very small units they would have found tenants as swiftly as the old camp had done. In Exeter, Devon County Council has developed a site of 12 nursery units of about 1000 square feet each. Modern standards necessitate rents which were in the region of £3.50 per square foot in 1982, or nearly £70 per week, and at that level little interest was shown. A large proportion of the available small scale would-be entrepreneurs cannot afford to start off in the sort of premises modern statutory standards dictate.

Heathpark Industrial Estate former Army Camp   Courtesy Exeter *Express and Echo*

A survey of private businesses in Honiton other than purely retail outlets was carried out in the winter of 1980–81.[1] Of 186 businesses

[1] A. Glyn-Jones *Small Firms in a Country Town*, (*op. cit.*) surveys Honiton businesses, reporting on their problems and prospects, employment offered, premises needed, areas served, motivation and skills of proprietors and relationship with local administration.

interviewed, comprising almost all of the non-retail private enterprise sector in the Borough and employing in all some 1,885 people, 94, offering employment to some 330 people, were operating in 1,500 square feet or less. Most of the firms (158 out of 186) and most of the employment (1,371 out of 1,885) are in properties away from the two estates. In terms of land use, the density of employment offered decreased as the size of the unit increased, with the county industrial estate working out at only about 14 people per acre — an eventuality which the county structure plan had expected, given the propensity for the estates to attract warehousing, and for the increased capital intensity of major manufacturing enterprises.

The multiplicity of small firms will no doubt suffer a high casualty rate, and local authority officers as well as councillors, ratepayers, and, one must assume, job seekers, would have preferred the presence of substantial enterprises offering security and stability. But they have not come, and the one substantial migrant firm which has been attracted cost the District over a quarter of a million pounds in subsidised loans. Substantial firms begin, however, as struggling insubstantial firms. Out of 150 locally-autonomous Honiton firms, sixteen now employ 11 to 20 people, 10 employ 21 to 50 and two employ over 50 people each. Of these 150 firms, 86 have been founded since 1964, 75 of which began life in, or within 20 miles of, Honiton (though at least 22 of them were founded by individuals who had come to the area as migrants from elsewhere in Britain).

Experience over recent years, when manufacturing industry has been shedding labour and vast established enterprises closing branches, has led to some revision of the earlier faith in industrial giants as the cornerstone of prosperity. Honiton's modest development has enabled the population to continue to increase, and the 1981 census showed a total population of 6,500, including an increase since 1971 of over 750 in those of working age. Statistics on the proportion who are economically active are not yet available — all that can be said is that the average 1981 unemployment rate at 10.6 per cent, was better than the national average of 11.4 per cent, (see Appendix 3) and given the qualifications about age discussed earlier in this chapter, the situation is probably in fact considerably better than average.

The Honiton business scene is probably not very affluent, and makes a greater contribution to job creation than to wealth creation. To return, however, to the discussion with which this chapter opened, it appears that Honiton has a good deal to offer in terms of quality of life. Its population increase is of the type identified by the OPCS *Population Trends Autumn 1981*, interpreting the 'counterurbanisation' evident in the census results, which stated 'population growth in the main will be strongly associated with smaller towns and accessible settlements in the countryside — the areas apparently most suited to economic growth'.

VII

THE STATUTORY PERSONAL SERVICES

With the extension, after World War II, of state responsibility for the provision of infrastructure and services, increased emphasis came to be placed on planning in the sense of timely and efficient investment in statutory undertakings; an activity which might equally well be called — and in private industry often is called — management. In a recent (1979) annual report of a major multi-national company, for instance, the chairman's statement remarks on two of 'the various necessary elements of management: the most efficient deployment of our financial resources; and the anticipation of social and economic changes, and our reaction to them in a socially responsible way' – a statement that could equally well describe comparable local government objectives.

Statutory planning had a further goal, more specific perhaps than the general aim of promoting prosperity which the last chapter discussed; and that was to co-ordinate the investment decisions of the responsible state authorities. This is clearly no small task, for it meant trying to harness the intentions not only of the various departments or separate authorities (many with planning and liaison staffs at regional, area, or district levels) dealing with housing, water, sewerage, education, health or transport, but also the problems and proposals of the Ministry of Agriculture, the Development Commission, COSIRA, and a group of ministers and civil servants in a fluctuating administrative amalgam called at various times the Board of Trade, Ministry of Power, Ministry of Technology, Department of Trade and Industry, and Department of Energy, not to mention the post-1970 Department of the Environment whose Secretary of State became the minister ultimately responsible for planning. To quote the *Strategic Settlement Pattern* published by the South West Economic Planning Council in 1975 after lengthy consultations:

> It must be the task of those authorities with statutory or other responsibilities to translate our broad recommendations into detailed policies and actions . . . we also consider that the strategy will be of value to other public authorities — such as water authorities, energy suppliers, the Post Office, the public transport sector — as indicating the broad long-term needs of the South West . . . .

A strategy for population settlement becomes of practical significance, as the above quotation implies, only when it is translated into specific investment decisions in a specific place at a specific time. Chapter V explored the impact of population assumptions on two crucial aspects of settlement: the provision of sewerage and the allocation of development land as designated in an outline development plan. It drew attention, too, to the fact that, for reasons of resource constraints as well as the fallibility of trend projections, the formal planning process, though couched in terms of a precise time-scale, cannot in fact offer the providers any assurance on when their services will be needed. This chapter will look at the initiatives that have been taken for the delivery of certain services in Honiton, and at the assessments which promoted them.

To cover the whole range of responsibilities is impossible. This chapter will concentrate on those services which entered into the formal planning process, being listed in the *County Development Plan* or the *Structure Plan*, or in one of the local outline development plans; in other words topics which are included within the specifically articulated goals. In the pre-1974 County Development Plans these were mainly limited to county or district responsibilities, but some NHS provision, i.e. hospitals, was included, as were trunk roads, a national not local responsibility. The *Structure Plan* gives specific details about health care and sewerage, both by then the responsibility of separate non-elected authorities, but is not specific about energy or telecommunications. There is also some amendment over time of the topics thought worthy of inclusion; community centres, for instance, figure in the first CDP but libraries do not. By 1964 this selection is reversed.

There is a difficulty in that it is not always clear whether the provision listed as intended by a certain date refers to a building or a function, and neither the records nor the people who could clarify this are in all cases now available for consultation. The Written Statement for the original 1959 CDP was itself troubled by this distinction in relation to community centres, and decided that any settlement having a hall provided for the general use of the community should be considered as having a community centre. There was in Honiton a privately-owned hall which the local authority leased, and has continued to do so. The functions of a maternity and child welfare clinic and of a regional library existed in Honiton throughout the period under review, but in both cases used non-purpose-built premises. The outline development plans elucidate, because they identify actual land-use proposals (see Figures 3, 4 and 5). The first, (for March 1968 when the County, though without District agreement, finalised the plan) shows sites for a proposed neighbourhood centre, health centre (a metamorphosis of the earlier intention to provide a clinic), ambulance station and primary school (in addition to the existing one). The 1974 review and accompanying town centre map identify sites for an intended old people's home, health centre, ambulance station, regional library, third primary school, two neighbourhood centres and a 'general purpose entertainment building'.

Two aspects of the formal planning process influenced the decisions made. Population projections were relevant to the decisions made by the library and education services; and the location of land designated for development influenced the health and education services. But other pressures were of sufficient strength to frustrate, or in some cases amend, avowed intentions as expressed in the plans.

The building of a new library at Honiton, together with a garage for the attached mobile library, was programmed for 1964/65, but in spite of anxious inspections in the early 1960s, no suitable site could be found at a price the service could afford, nor did any of the existing available buildings prove suitable. The mobile library was garaged in a bay of the Civil Defence headquarters, but by the mid-1960s the main library's problems were critical, for the lease on its temporary building was expiring without prospect of renewal. In 1966, when the Civil Defence group asked if their bay was still needed, the service had to reply that 'owing to government financial restrictions and difficulties we are having in obtaining a site for the proposed new library at Honiton, there seems to be little chance of new premises being built in the next year or two'. The library next found temporary shelter in the offices of the Honiton Municipal Borough Council, where it remained for three years until given notice to go by the Council, partly on the grounds that they wanted the space for themselves, partly because a visit from the Factory Inspectorate had told them the washing facilities were inadequate, and the Council had no intention of spending money to improve them.

During these three years the service endeavoured to develop a site jointly with first Devon's Health Committee and then the Police, but when both these possible partnerships fell through, the Library Service had to cry off, since 'expenditure of this size cannot be justified on a site for a library, even in normal financial conditions, but of course in the present [1967] economic crisis the sum of money would not be approved either by the County Council or by the appropriate Ministry'. The next temporary solution was a hut on a site bought but not yet used for an extension to the Magistrate's Courts, and tenancy of this site continued for the next five or six years. Meanwhile, in 1970, the opportunity occurred to obtain a central site belonging to the East Devon Water Board, who were moving to Exeter. There was no room on the site for the mobile library, nevertheless it seemed the best available prospect, and a 2,900 square foot library was designed for a projected 1981 population of 9,000, at an estimated cost of £33,700. By the middle of 1971 it was decided, in view of the Planning Department's estimate of a population of 10,000 by 1991, to extend the building to 3,600 square feet, which the County Architect commented was still '20 per cent below Department of Education and Science standards'. This extension, plus inflation, resulted in a rapid escalation of the estimate, and by October 1973 the cost was estimated at £70,030. It was opened in 1975.

With the 1981 population now known to be about 6,500, it seems unlikely that the 1991 forecast will be reached, so the size of library actually established may well prove adequate longer than was expected. The 1974 *Honiton Review*, envisaging a population of 10,000 in 1991, had postulated the inclusion of a small branch library in one of the neighbourhood centres. The main determinant of the library's position and extent seems to have been the necessity to find a reasonably central site coupled with the constraints imposed by costs.

The fortunes of the proposed Health Centre responded to somewhat more complex pressures. A school clinic had existed beside Honiton School since the 1950s, and in 1967 this was transferred from Devon County's Education Committee to the same Authority's Health Committee, who took over responsibility for outstanding loan charges. By the time of the 1969 Review of the *County Development Plan* the decision had been taken, and was incorporated in the plan, to supersede the clinic with a Health Centre, including surgery accommodation for all the town's doctors. In the winter of 1969/70 the County bought a centre-town site, Black Lion Fields, adjacent to a site where they had already in the mid-1960s built a home for the elderly mentally infirm. The site and its intended use were duly incorporated in the outline development plans of 1968/69 and 1974.

Public meetings in the town in the early 1970s revealed that neither the local people nor the local doctors welcomed the idea. Among local people there emerged a distrust of what they suspected would tend towards 'supermarket medicine', and the doctors, for their part, were not at that stage attracted by the idea. The site itself, though central, had several problems. It was not large, there would be little parking space, and if ambulances were housed on the ground floor, as initial proposals suggested, all other facilities would have to be on higher floors dependent on the awkwardness of stairs or lifts. The proposals were abandoned, and when the 1974 reorganisation of county and NHS functions occurred, it was the original rather small school clinic that was passed to the NHS — the new site remained county property. Though overcrowded, the clinic still provides such services as chiropody, audiometry, ante-natal and baby care, family planning and the premises for the school dental and eye services.

Over the following years the doctors resolved their objections, and decided to set up a shared headquarters. They chose a site beside the hospital, where they opened in 1978, health visitors and community nurses operating from these premises. The doctors were influenced in their choice of site by its proximity to the area where the outline development plan had specified new residential development would be

61

located, towards the south and west of the town. This consideration outweighed, in their opinion, the fact that the site was up a hill. To mitigate the ill-effects of this, the doctors organised a minibus service for a while, but it was little used and was ultimately discontinued. The premises, which were financed by the doctors with help from the General Practice Finance Corporation, were constructed in consultation with the Health Authority, who requested the development to be done in such a way that later expansion would be possible. There is no present plan to expand.

In the pre-reorganisation days, when the County provided the Ambulance Service, via the agency of the St John Ambulance Brigade in Honiton, it had been the intention to provide a new station. A site in Dowell Street had been bought for this purpose, and the site and its intended use are recorded in both outline development plans. Difficulties arose over the use of the site because of archaeological discoveries, and although the site was transferred to the NHS in 1974, the new Authority accepted an offer of temporary space at the local hospital, though the vehicles had to be garaged in the open. After Heathpark Army camp became available, the intention was to relocate there, and a half-hectare site was allocated by East Devon District Council. But capital investment restrictions meant that in the winter of 1979/80 the proposal had to be abandoned. A Devon County highways depot in Dowell Street became surplus to requirements, however, and the Ambulance Service has been able to lease those premises and at a modest £12,000 to adapt them to its own use. The original Ambulance Station site remains unused.

The Social Services Department also had intentions the land-use implications of which were incorporated in the outline development plans. It was intended to set up a social service office associated with the Health Centre in Black Lion Fields, and the 1974 Town Centre Map incorporated this proposal, which failed with the demise of the Health Centre – the site is still used for allotments. After some uncertain sojourns under an annual tenancy, the Department in 1978 agreed to buy the old Borough Council offices (where the library had found shelter in the late 1960s). Late in 1978 they took possession.

The Social Services Department had staked out another site on the 1974 Town Centre Map for use as an old people's home, but the proposal itself dated back several years before that. Discussions about developing the site in conjunction with the old Borough Council had been going on at least since 1968, with proposals for both a county home and warden-controlled borough bungalows. In 1971 the County told the Borough they did not expect to *use* the site before 1973/76, probably not until 1976/77, but in 1972 they said that they were intending to proceed with the purchase.

In August 1973 the Department of Health and Social Security

notified local authorities that within six months they wanted a complete picture of the authority's intentions over the next ten years. A 15 page document set out guidelines of the sort of information that was wanted, and 20 pages of forms were provided. The document set out staffing targets for instance for social workers, home helps, day centre staff and the staff of residential homes; and targets for the delivery of such services as meals-on-wheels, daycare for children, the elderly and the mentally handicapped, community services for the mentally ill, and day and residential services for the mentally ill, calculated according to a formula related to expected population change. The report, with the confidence that only those well distanced from practical realities can manifest, remarked that

> the preparation of realistic forecasts of social services provision will require other local authority functions to be taken into account — housing, environmental planning and education — and also the activities of the health services and the voluntary sector. Planning in relation to personal social service provision of all kinds, field work and domiciliary support services, day services and residential care — will need to take into account, as far as possible, services and facilities that are, or in due course can be, provided by other bodies, whether independently or under formal or informal agreement with the local authority — e.g. to reserve places for it, with financial support from it on an agency basis. Consultation within each authority and (where responsibility rests elsewhere) with other local authorities, with hospital authorities and executive councils, and with national and local voluntary organisations which have relevant interests will therefore be called for.

Quite apart from the practicalities of such an exercise it was hardly a propitious moment to embark on it, with only eight months to go before local authority reorganisation brought a new structure into being. The Association of County Councils protested, and Devon County Social Services Committee demurred, asking at least to be allowed more time, but were refused. Preliminary analysis swiftly revealed that, even allowing for a ten per cent annual growth in real resources, which the document suggested was a reasonable assumption, there was no prospect whatever of affording the targets stipulated; and furthermore the ten per cent growth rate was itself double the figure envisaged for local authority expenditure in a recent government white paper.

However, a ten-year capital building programme was devised, covering *inter alia* the construction of some 14 old people's homes, that for Honiton being scheduled for 1976/77. Just before the programme was submitted, the sites team were asked to report on progress over the purchase of the land.

Within less than a year the economic disruptions that began with the Yom Kippur war had intervened. By the summer of 1974 four schemes in the capital programme had to be dropped, though they had already

63

received DHSS approval. Demand for social service provision was increasing by about 10 per cent per annum, and Devon County Council saw no way of exceeding a five per cent real growth rate. The Social Services Department appealed to Whitehall for help, only to be told that negotiations on the Rate Support Grant might well result in no provision for growth at all. In acceding to the next demand from the DHSS for a long-term capital investment forecast, the County Secretary warned that 'no capital programme can be anything but a guess, and may well be significantly wrong if local government is to contract its expenditure still further . . . I do not think', he added, 'that much weight should be given to the information contained in these forms, as the eventual programme will probably vary considerably from it, in the same way as the returns made about a year ago proved, as anticipated, to be pretty valueless.'

By July 1975 the DHSS itself was sending out reviews of the 1974/75 capital programme following further reductions in public expenditure announced by the Chancellor of the Exchequer in April. The County Secretary's forebodings proved all too well grounded. None of the 14 old people's homes was, in the event, to be built.

During 1975 East Devon District Council, inheritors of the Borough's interest in a joint scheme, made enquiries as to the likely future use of the land, still designated for an old people's home on the outline development plan but never in fact purchased by the County. Early in 1976 they were advised that the County was not in a position to consider the development within the foreseeable future, and the County's involvement was therefore withdrawn. The County retains ownership of the land adjacent to its earlier old people's home, and could use it, if it becomes feasible to do so, since all the purposes for which the land was originally earmarked have accommodated themselves elsewhere.

Educational building intentions, thought not unaffected, were less bedevilled by financial constraints than social services, since children enjoy a statutory right to schooling. Expectations, as signified in the first County Development Plan of 1959, were that the existing primary and secondary school would suffice until 1971, nor did the first review, valid till 1981, signify any change in that assessment. By 1967 however it was evident that a new primary school was needed, and the proposal was put forward as a second priority for the 1969/70 programme. In 1969 it received DES approval, one of only two to do so out of nine projects put forward. The school, 160 places as the first phase of a proposed 320-place school, opened in 1971. Its siting was determined with direct reference to the area in the outline development plan where residential development was planned and was indeed taking place. Though originally intended as a mixed infants and junior school, it opened as an infants school, juniors being expected to attend the existing town centre primary school until a second new school for juniors was built. The 1969 second review of the CDP listed the intention to provide these two schools in the period up to 1991. In fact however the influx of infants was less than expected, so the new school admitted juniors as well.

The problem then arose of the timing for the new (junior) school, or for the second phase of the recently built school. Many sources feed into the statistics on which estimates of future numbers are based. Dealing, as this prediction must, with an age group for which decennial census figures rapidly cease to apply, the OPCS population statistics are of little value, and prognostications of trends in the birthrate have been shown by bitter experience to be highly fallible. Education welfare officers can give some idea of how many local mothers are expecting new babies, but cuts in the establishment, and hence knowledge, of officers have made their assessments less valid. The Area Health Authority gives some guidance on the numbers of pre-school children in the area, based on immunisation and vaccination records, but these too are fallible due to a population mobility of about 20 per cent. The most reliable figures come from within the schools, but this can only trace the size of classes as they move up the school, it cannot predict new intake.

In a county like Devon, on the receiving end of migrational movement, new housing development is an obvious source of presumed recruitment into the schools. In 1975 the Education Department were complaining of the difficulty in obtaining 'housing information of any precision', and a system of close liaison was established between the County and the Districts whereby the Districts kept the County informed by means of a five-year rolling assessment of future development (see Appendix 7). Assessing its usefulness requires also a knowledge of actual completions. There was a long-standing arrangement for the pre-1974 district councils to notify the County of completions, and the new County Council in 1976 endeavoured to institute a firm system of notification from the new districts. But there were hiccoughs in the system, and the county officers were dubious whether the records they were amassing were accurate. Reconnaisance on the ground in Honiton in 1978 showed that the records were a serious understatement, by about 60 houses in two years, 36 per cent of the total, and the records had to be retrospectively amended, using electoral registers as a guide to completion dates. The figures for housing completions in Appendix 4 incorporate these adjustments, but the precise allocation of completions between 1976 and 1977 is not known. Comparisons of projections with actuality can only be made for the four years 1978 to 1981. Over these four years, as is evident from a comparison of Appendices 4 and 7, the projected aggregate proved very accurate — 222 completions against a projection of 215; though the projected distribution between private and local authority housing is not borne out by events, and the discrepancies become more marked in

65

the forecasts made in subsequent years. It is too early to say how much reliance can be placed on these figures, for, as Chapter V showed, many permissions are for various reasons not implemented.

Given likely completion figures, the Department then applies a formula which assumes a stable relationship between new housing and new children. The formula has varied over time with, for instance, the decline in the birthrate, but even so it has proved somewhat rough-and-ready. Door to door surveys on particular estates have yielded widely different harvests of young children. In an approach to the Planning Department late in 1978 the Education Department mentioned their interest in 'good and early information about the population which we might expect the new [Honiton] development to produce', but there is no indication that the planners have any better tools for diagnosis than the Education Department are already using. Some useful advice comes from the Department's own sites and buildings staff who are able to keep a weather eye on the sort of changes taking place on the ground.

Recent observations in East Devon have suggested that the overall effect of new housing in terms of increasing pressure on the schools is much less than had been expected, perhaps because it is coupled with the indigenous effects of the decline in the birthrate. The primary school population in Devon looks like dropping by about 25 per cent over the period 1974 to 1985, indeed Devon now has more primary places than pupils, but fresh provision is still likely to be needed, since the places may well not be where the children are.

Planning in the necessary good time on the basis of development permissions involves the risk, as Chapter V has pointed out, that the development may not go ahead, or not on the expected time scale. So far as the future of Honiton is concerned, educational planning is proceeding on the assumption that the extensive permissions granted will indeed be implemented, and that this will add to pressures in the vicinity of the newer school. Given that pressure on the town centre school has been dropping, it is doubtful whether there is going to be a need in the foreseeable future for the second new primary school postulated in the 1969 review of the CDP, and indicated in the outline development plan, though the County's interest in a prospective site is not being terminated. There are problems, however, particularly in the maintenance of socio-economic balance, in re-allocating catchment areas between the two existing primary schools.

By 1978/79 pressure on the newer primary school had reached the point at which a temporary mobile classroom had to be assigned to it, and in the light of the further acreages allocated for development, it was decided to apply for DES permission to implement Phase 2, and build for a further 160 places at the school. The submission has been made without high priority, as a proposal for the 1985/86 major building programme.

66

The calculation of numbers at secondary school level is simplified to the extent that on the timescales involved the birthrate is not of practical significance, and much guidance is available from the numbers in the primary schools. Investment decisions were complicated, however, by two initiatives in social policy which had not been introduced at the time both the original *County Development Plan* and its first review were content to list Honiton's secondary modern school and leave it at that. One was the raising of the school leaving age, the other was the objective of establishing comprehensive education. The Honiton Secondary School, built in 1940, had served since the 1944 Act as a secondary modern school, with some 25 per cent of local children attending grammar school in Ottery St Mary which also served the grammar school needs of the Sidmouth area. No one school, therefore, could be reorganised without repercussions on all three towns.

The school was able to meet the expansion arising from the raising of the school leaving age, which came into effect in 1973, by building extensions. The proposal to make Honiton school a comprehensive dates from the mid-Sixties, and led to a corresponding amendment to the *County Development Plan*, the second review of which substituted 'one comprehensive (junior dept.)' for the existing secondary modern. Among proposed new schools it listed a new comprehensive by 1991, but as there has never been a suggestion that the town could sustain two comprehensive schools, this presumably refers to intended rehabilitation of the existing secondary modern school buildings.

The fact that the plan lists a junior department school only (seniors over 14 were to go to Ottery) pinpoints the problem in the area which was to result in the passage of a further 13 years before comprehensive reorganisation was to be introduced. A viable VIth form was held to require 100 pupils in order to provide for a full range of staffing, and for groups large enough for stimulating discussions among peers. Given the assumption that about 40 per cent might stay on into the VIth form, that required an intake of at least six or seven forms — 180 to 210 children at 30 per form. Smaller schools might have their advantages, but against them must be set the choice of fewer VIth form options and the possibility that there might have to be some joint tuition of first and second year VIth formers. So the solution proposed for Honiton and Sidmouth was to have junior schools only and send the older children to Ottery.

The proposal was not welcomed in Sidmouth or Honiton. While discussions continued in the late Sixties and early Seventies population was building up within all the catchment areas, with the result that by the mid-1970s it seemed feasible to propose that only the VIth form pupils should go to Ottery, with Sidmouth and Honiton each providing a full 11–16 education. The Governors of Honiton school, strongly backed by local opinion, stated their preference for an 11–18 school, and the County compromised by accepting the idea of an 11–17 school, though this was not for A-levels but rather for those wishing to extend or resit Os and CSEs. Much investment in building would be required, both to extend the non-academic options at Ottery, and to provide for the more academic options at Honiton and Sidmouth.

The original 1940 school was intended for about 250 pupils, but by 1960 numbers had climbed to 689, though there was a big reduction six years later when Ottery's non-grammar stream were switched from Honiton to Sidmouth, a transition which took a full school generation to complete, as those who had started at Honiton finished their schooling there. But numbers again began to build, and by 1976 were back to 685. Throughout the period extensive use had to be made of temporary mobile classrooms, the only permanent buildings to be added being the ROSLA block in 1972–73. (By late 1979 no less than 18 temporary classrooms were in use.) Thus quite apart from all the extra investment to provide the full range of options which comprehensive reorganisation should secure, deficiencies in 'basic needs' were also manifest. Already by March 1975 the Education Committee were discussing proposals for a 150-place extension at the school. About 10 villages were 'feeding' Honiton, and numbers in the relevant primary schools were known. The problem, as with the primary schools, was to assess the likely impact of new housing, not merely in Honiton but throughout the catchment area.

New housing was not expected to produce a secondary school population comparable to its primary level product, and the formula applied in 1975 was 0.1 child per house, or one child to every ten houses, though this was increased the next year to three children per 20 houses. The year 1975 preceded the efforts made to refine housing information, and forward planning was having to proceed on rather vague assumptions. Documents comment 'no firm plans are known, but there is a strong possibility that 200 council houses will be built by 1980 plus about 100 private'. The same figure of 300 overall is arrived at in another assessment which remarks that there are planning permissions approved for at least 630 houses in the area — but the rate of take-up is unknown. A guesstimate of 300 houses by 1980 is proposed. The upshot was that approval was sought and obtained from the DES for a 90-place extension, which was programmed for 1978/79. Cost escalation ensured that the estimate of £122,000 made in 1976 was subjected to rapid upward revisions, and by the end of 1978 had reached over £286,000. Within a year the total cost for the 90-place extension by then under construction had reached £348,000. The plans incorporated many elements to smooth the path to comprehensive reorganisation, including a science block and three laboratories.

The precise form that re-organisation was to take remained undetermined. Since local government reorganisation in 1974 the three

68

affected towns had ceased to be independent local authorities, and all formed part of the East Devon District. This altered the political complexion, for although Districts were not and had never been responsible for education, a Sidmouth District councillor was also Chairman of the County Council Education Committee, and was particularly keen to see all three towns possessed of comprehensive schools with 'parity of esteem'. Meetings of staff, governors and parents in the area tended strongly to back this view, stressing the advantages of relatively small schools, and the enhanced sense of community to be expected from the presence of a local school serving the entire secondary span. There was also the saving in travel costs to be thrown into the equation, a substantial consideration since transport costs had begun their ineluctable climb.

Numbers were of the essence; not merely total pupils numbers in the area, as signified by existing primary schools and by housing forecasts, but there was yet another variable — the proportion of pupils likely to stay on to provide a viable VIth form. A submission from representatives of several teaching unions held that in a rural comprehensive the proportion staying on was likely to be nearer 50 per cent than the 'formula figure' of 40 per cent (though there seems room for some ambiguity here, for earlier figures of those expected to stay on from the old secondary modern stream seemed to envisage them extending their range of Os and CSEs rather than sharing A-level work). On this basis, the teachers suggested that even if there were no further growth of population — and on the contrary further development was certainly expected at Honiton — the catchment areas of the three towns would produce a 15-form entry each year. They held to the view that three 'parity of esteem' schools were feasible.

Consultations were held with parents of primary school children about their preferences. At this stage, in 1979, a new element entered the calculations. Instead of the rolling five-year forecast of housing completions, future numbers were calculated on the basis not of known development proposals, but of the acreages allocated for future development in the period of the Structure Plan — i.e. to 1991. This involved applying a formula for housing density per acre as well as child density per house, and it meant that the child densities had to be assumed before there was any evidence available of the type of development to be pursued. Given the various assumptions, a prognostication was reached of an annual intake of about 215 at Honiton, a 7-form entry; 125 at Ottery, a 4-form entry; and 145 at Sidmouth, a 5-form entry. It was recognised that Sidmouth and Ottery were on the small side, and might need extra resources to be made available, but against this possible extra demand had to be set a probable saving of £95,000 a year in transport costs — less a small sum to cover individual VIth formers who might need to travel to one of the

69

other schools, or even to colleges at Exeter or Tiverton, in pursuit of a particular option. Each school was considered large enough to allow for 12 or more subjects at A-level, and judging by the results of a national survey, that would cater for some 85 per cent of desired options.

By the end of May 1979 a further small source of pupils for Ottery had been uncovered in a convent, and the even more optimistic assumption was being made of a 55 per cent stay-on-rate into the VIth form. In June 1979 the Education Committee agreed the proposals. The gross cost for extensions and adaptations at Honiton school was estimated at £985,000, including a further extension of 150 places plus adaptations at a cost calculated in 1981 at about £606,000. In January 1980 the intention was made public for Honiton to be a comprehensive school catering for about 1000 children and serving some 12 catchment villages. By the end of the year the Secretary of State had given final approval.

In September 1982 the three schools will accept their first comprehensive intake, with Sidmouth and Honiton functioning as 11–17 schools for the first few years, while the intake works its way up to the top of the school. The extensions at Honiton should be completed by February 1984. At Ottery, meanwhile, some half million pounds has been budgeted for extensions including the craft block, new laboratories and an art and music teaching block; and in May 1983 it is hoped to open extensions at Sidmouth costing nearly £400,000 and providing new laboratories, and rooms for art, music, home economics and dressmaking.

Only time will tell how near the mark these calculations prove to be, but at least each town will have a fine school. Educational planners are well aware that the application of simple formulae equating housing with child numbers is highly fallible. Since the decision was made there has been a change in the allocation of residential land at Ottery. Under the 1964 County Development Plan, Ottery was scheduled to become a 'sub-urban centre', but the enlargement envisaged met with so much resistance when the proposed outline development plan was subsequently being discussed that much more modest acreages for development were determined upon, and a proposed new primary school included in the 1964 plan was expunged from the 1969 review (though there was a major enlargement to the infant school in 1974). By the time of the Structure Plan in 1979, Ottery was among towns where expenditure on infrastructure was to be curtailed in view of the greater priorities elsewhere, and land for development was reduced to 10 acres, at which level no significant input into the school was allowed for in the figures quoted above. However, a subsequent amendment trebled the acreage to 30, an extra 200 houses yielding 20 children on recent density assumptions. This would be a welcome addition, since Ottery had the smallest school potential.

The question remains as to what time-scale will apply. Late in 1977 the school building programme was considering the impact of consent for a mass 400-plus houses in the small village of Dunkeswell (one of those feeding pupils to Honiton) where there was not even a primary school. Construction was expected to start in January 1978, but to date only about 20 houses have been built. The permissions were granted under the provisions of the old County Development Plan which in 1969 added Dunkeswell to the list of key settlements, but by the time of the Structure Plan it no longer appeared that this role was appropriate. The planning permission cannot be rescinded except at unacceptable cost in compensation, but there is no present indication that demand will support extensive further construction. This acreage, accordingly, seems unlikely to produce many new children. On the other hand, however, the impact of unemployment on school-leavers may well tempt higher proportions to stay on into the VIth form.

This chapter has examined some of the practical problems faced in achieving the delivery of a range of statutory services. It reveals that the objective of rational co-ordinated forward planning has, at the practical level, been undermined by the familiar gremlins of resource shortages, human awkwardness, and the unpredictability of future needs. Administrators have had to improvise, adapt, and stay alert to unscheduled opportunities — in short to 'fly by the seat of their pants' to an extent more often associated with the entrepreneur than the bureaucrat. Nor does experience suggest that in this respect the future will be very different from the past.

VIII

FUTURE CONDITIONAL

The old development plans were principally concerned with sound management, both of land and of resources; the key settlement policy, for instance, was an attempt to service rural communities and discourage urban sprawl rather than an implied judgement about the values of rural or urban life. Past statistics and their likely significance for the future were sufficient justification for the proposals made. The new structure plans, with their social and economic objectives, have not only required more explicit interpretation and justification for the policy conclusions reached, they have also implied a scale of values.

The combination of projected trends, conjectural modifications of trends and political aspirations has proved a hazardous guide, and it is astonishing looking back over the years covered by this study, how rapid and how drastic have been the changes in the assumptions on which the various plans and studies were based.

Man's anxiety to know the future is perennial. Babylonians employed stargazers for the task; the Romans read entrails. Modern methods begin with the extrapolation of statistics and the projection of trends. People, their number and location, have been a crucial ingredient in all the planning documents quoted throughout this study. Barring a catastrophe such as nuclear war, demographic prognostications may be accurate enough so far as those already born are concerned, though even here doctors maintain that survival rates, for example, (and therefore our assumptions about, e.g., pensioner numbers) could be quickly and sharply affected by a big change in smoking habits. Even so, great problems remain for the planners, who, if they are to estimate the appropriate housing and ancillary provision for any particular settlement, have to make assumptions about future household sizes, net family formation or the rate and direction of internal migration. When it comes to estimating the birthrate, with all that is implied for the provision of maternity wards, midwives, primary schools, or teachers, experience has proved chastening. For instance, the projected figure for live births in the United Kingdom in 1995 differed by over a million between the 1955 and 1965 forecasts, and even for the much closer, and therefore more relevant, date of 1975, the variation amounted to almost half a million. The expected increase of 20 million in population between 1965 and 2000, a cardinal assumption of the National Plan and of the AIC reports and their progeny in the

72

mid-Sixties, had by 1982 been progressively revised to less than four million over the same period.

The validity of economic forecasts has proved even more fragile, though some sort of assumptions have to be made, not only because providing infrastructure, from sewage systems to new London airports or channel tunnels cost tax money, and have to be budgeted for, but also because assessments are needed — of likely levels of car or second-home ownership for instance, for the planning of roads or residential land; or of the extent to which per capita demand for energy or water may rise, necessitating appropriate provision of reservoirs or power stations. The task of forecasting is not in essence different from that facing private industry, with the exception that misjudgements, given the cost, complexity and time-lag of modern technology, can bankrupt private industry, whereas the extent of mis-allocation of funds by the state is less dramatically advertised. An illustration of the uncertainties is provided by the Department of Energy's October 1982 projections of energy use over the next 30 years, which produced eight different scenarios, based *inter alia* on two energy price assumptions and three economic growth assumptions, producing assessments varying from a decline of five per cent to an increase of 33 per cent in demand by the end of the century. The President of Royal Dutch Petroleum was recently quoted[1] as saying 'we simply do not know what will happen — not even between now and the year end.'

Forecasts can be falsified by many factors, political social or technological. For instance, many of the large vessels of the British fishing fleet were built in the 1960s with no apprehension that the Cod War would force them into waters where their operation would be uneconomic. Calculations about the cost and productivity of generating stations have been vitiated, not only by unexpected technical problems, but by factors such as labour disputes — in 1976 nearly 30 per cent of available working time at the Isle of Grain power station construction site was lost in 'industrial action'. The Concorde project, launched in the expectation of selling 400 planes was turned into fiasco by the escalation in oil prices and the introduction of the Jumbo Jet, with the result that sales barely reached double figures. One of the saddest planning disasters was the construction at huge expense of the Hunterston and Portavadie yards for the building of concrete oil drilling platforms — sad because not only did they never obtain an order, oil technology having changed by the time they were ready, but the development of Portavadie was approved in the face of a consultant's report to the Government recommending that the land involved should form part of a conservation area.[2] Its accompanying

[1] *The Times*, 13 October 1982.
[2] Jack Holmes Planning Group (1974) A Report to the Government on the Physical, Economic and Social Aspects of locating additional platform construction yards round the UK coast.

village, never occupied, was disposed of to 'a foreign buyer' in 1980, at a fraction of its cost.

Out of these failures in foresight and achievement has stemmed an increasing preoccupation with 'futurology'. Earlier planning placed heavy reliance on the projection of trends, but the one certain propensity of trends is that sooner or later most will change. A multiplicity of hypotheses can be introduced to account, and provide, for change, and the speed of modern computers makes it feasible to explore the notional effects of such hypotheses. It does not, however, determine which hypothesis is likely to be correct. Planners are still faced with 'choosing a scenario', a combination of present facts and future hopes intershot with further assumptions about the likely impact of changes which the authorities themselves intend to set in train.

The difficulties facing planners in both public and private undertakings have become a subject with its own literature analysing uncertainty and proposing new institutions to deal with it, such as the abortive 1977 proposals from the Director of the London School of Economics for a British counterpart to the Brookings Institution of Washington. Awareness of demographic difficulties came to a head in the mid-1970s, when it became impossible to ignore the fact that a long expected increase in the birthrate was in fact being replaced by a decline. Studies began to emerge from a number of sources, including the Government's own Central Policy Review Staff, questioning prevailing assumptions about the numbers of doctors or teachers needed, and calling for more flexibility in the deployment of resources for social policy. The Social Science Research Council report for 1976–77 pleaded for a better understanding of the factors influencing population size, and the Centre for Studies in Social Policy, at about the same time, published in *The Uncertain Future* a collection of papers by academics and senior administrators in Britain and the Netherlands, the message of which is summed up in the title of the first paper: 'the certainty of the uncertain future'.

In the economic sphere, in 1979 a number of contributors working within the private sector combined to write *Planning in an Age of Uncertainty*, published by *The Financial Times*, which began with the assertion 'Planning is just a waste of time nowadays — especially so-called strategic planning. In today's world there's no point looking further forward than a one- or two-year budget.' The succeeding papers were less pessimistic, but the shortening of horizons was constantly stressed, whether it was businessmen retracting 'from, say, five to three years', or even more cautious, looking 'sometimes only six or 12 months ahead'. At Westminster, meanwhile, a member of the Environmental Sub-Committee of the Expenditure Committee was speculating, in 1977 'whether structure plans serve any useful purpose at all'.

In addition to these forecasting difficulties, theories of cause and effect change over time. In the mid-Sixties the AIC report, for instance, particularly decried the multiplicity in Devon of firms with fewer than 20 employees; of self-employment and part-time work; and of the high number of relatively small farms. Recent work in America, however, has claimed that the principal job generators have been firms with fewer than 20 employees;[1] by the late Seventies and early Eighties part-time working and self-generated employment were being lauded as appropriate responses to the decline of employment in obsolescent industries, to such an extent that by the autumn of 1980 even the well-established theory of zoning was under fire in DOE Circular 22/80, which pleaded for elasticity to help small enterprises in residential zones. With the increasing substitution, in new industries, of technology for manpower, the insistence of the Sixties on the value of manufacturing as a generator of employment has been replaced by an emphasis on services.[2]

The Sixties was also the high-tide of the belief that economic prosperity could best be generated by concentrating development on the major conurbations, whether or not this was ideal from other points of view. This approach was propounded in the AIC reports and supported by SWEPC's *Region with a Future*. There was much difference of opinion in county council committees about this belief, discussion centring on whether to concentrate development on Plymouth, or seek to disperse it to the leading towns and villages. An amendment to achieve the second alternative was defeated at a council meeting on 19 October 1967. So far did opinion change over the next ten years however, that by the time the Structure Plan was submitted to the Secretary of State a new section on industries in rural areas had been inserted, not only accepting the establishment of 'units of employment' which accorded with the character of the locality, but even permitting employment development *outside* settlements where 'special justification' could be shown, and subject to the adequacy of services and the protection of the landscape. The Development Commission are also less concerned with selected locations as defined in statutory plans, and are anxious to see workshops develop virtually wherever craftsmen are capable of earning a living. Even the assumption that farm holdings should be amalgamated and larger concentrations encouraged — a cardinal principle with the EEC at one time — has been superseded in Europe by a recognition of the social benefits of an agriculturally-based population, by the appointment of agricultural 'socio-economic advisers', and by the search for methods of boosting smallholder incomes by tourism or part-time industrial work (plus, or course, the CAP!) rather than sending farmers from the land to swell the city jobless.

[1]David L. Birch, *The Job Generation Process* (M.I.T., 1979).
[2]See for instance Graeme Shankland, *Our Secret Economy* (Anglo-German Foundation) 1980.

When the key settlement policy was promulgated in the 1964 review of the County Development Plan, it was as a means of coping with the need for services of a scattered and declining rural population. In fact, the century-long movement from rural to urban areas was, it now appears, beginning to reverse. The 'counter-urbanisation' trend probably began in the 1960s[1] but did not register statistically until the 1981 census, which revealed a movement of population, not only in Devon but elsewhere, into the more as well as the less remote rural areas. The hierarchic settlement policy had been disliked by some of the districts, both before and after local government reorganisation. East Devon District Council was among those voicing opposition as recently as the discussions in preparation for the Structure Plan, when they pointed out that in endeavouring to arrest rural decline (which was not in aggregate still occurring, but the available statistics were out of date) they were trying to sustain some 60 villages. These and similar pressures led to revisions of the draft structure plan, which accepted provision of housing in villages subject to the scale being acceptable and to services being available. By the time the Secretary of State approved the plan, the attitude to village development had been even further modified permitting development, whether of homes or jobs, outside the list of classified settlements, wherever infrastructure was available or *could be provided at small cost*. The 1981 census was to reveal that population had in fact been dispersing itself widespread across the County and was not restricted to any particular area or type of settlement.

If human aspirations are defined sufficiently vaguely — in terms of the search for the 'good life' for instance, or the pursuit of happiness — then these changes may well represent no more than new ways of seeking old goals. Even so, the shifts in perceived needs may be radical enough to qualify as a change of dominant values. In *Great Planning Disasters*[2] Peter Hall inclined to the view that among the most challenging aspects of planning were these shifts in people's scale of values. He explored the trinity of uncertainties first adumbrated by Friend and Jessop in 1969:[3] uncertainty about the relevant environment (UE) e.g. the size of the birthrate; uncertainty about related decisions (UR), i.e. decisions being made outside the scope of the immediate decision, but having a potential influence; and uncertainty about value judgements (UV), which could vary not only from group to group, but in the same group over a period of time. Frequently, he points out, what seems to be a UE or a UR problem, turns out on closer analysis to be UV.

[1]A.G. Champion, *Counterurbanisation and rural rejuvenation in rural Britain* (University of Newcastle upon Tyne, Geography Department, 1981).
[2]P. Hall *Great Planning Disasters* (Weidenfield & Nicholson, London, 1980).
[3]Friend, J. K. and Jessop, W.N., *The Government and Strategic Choice* (Tavistock Publications, 1969).

An example of the complications of UV changes is the long-drawn out saga, which Hall uses in his catalogue of disasters, of the London Ringway road system. He says:

> The strange irony is that all the proponents still claim that their chief concern is with the quality of life of the archetypal average Londoner. Their visions of what make up the good life are very different, and to some extent they represent a *Zeitgeist*. The good future life of the early 1960s consisted in ceaseless mobility in search of an ever widening range of choice in jobs, education, entertainment and social life. The good future life of the early 1970s was seen in almost the reverse trend of life; in a small, place bounded, face-to-face community . . .[1].

Reference was made in Chapter VI to the fact that the late Sixties saw the end of the consensus that economic growth was normal, a belief assailed from two quarters, those who questioned whether the consequences of growth were necessarily benign; and those, perhaps far more numerous, who questioned whether its continuation was feasible. These attitudes had become significant, and organisations such as Friends of the Earth and the Conservation Society had sprung to prominence even before the 1973 energy crisis imposed awareness on even the most sanguine.

The cover of the Exeter sub-regional study[2] of 1975 featured traffic on the motorway's six lanes crossing a railway line on which a train was speeding along. To that extent it breathed the authentic spirit of Sixties mobility. But the text was beginning to incorporate several themes which, if not themselves symptomatic of changing values, were certainly congruent with a new *Zeitgeist*. The study's discussions of car ownership, for instance, are tempered with references to inflation in the costs of private motoring and the possible implications for public transport and the siting of commuters. The interest demonstrated in planning documents over the years in the quality of agricultural land is now enhanced by references to the cost of imported foodstuffs and the relevance of the White Paper *Food from our own Resources*.

The safeguarding of food-producing land emerged as one of the overriding concerns voiced during the public consultations preceding the formulation of the Structure Plan. Linked as it was with pleas to preserve 'the Devon environment' or 'scenic landscapes,' this may be no more than a new way in which to express distrust of urbanisation and of migrant hordes of non-Devonians — an attitude which, in the form of objections to overspill, had rumbled on in county committees of the Sixties, culminating in the specific resolution of rejection in 1969. The Devon Conservation Forum's 1976 paper *Urbanisation in Devon* urgently insisted that planning existed to arbitrate between the individual's

[1] *Great Planning Disasters*, p. 86.
[2] *Towards 2001 op. cit.*

desires (e.g. to move to Devon) and the common good, which might well require both the preservation of food-producing land and the protection of the Devon environment as a recreation and holiday area.

Half the town and parish councils returning comments during the Structure Plan consultation process were opposed to further development, but in company with the 80 per cent of individuals replying who stressed the need for more housing, they wanted improved job-provision, specifically light, agriculture-based, or craft industry. The County's summary of these responses commented drily on the extent to which 'the inevitable contradictions between objectives may not be apparent at this stage'. The 1981 census, however, has indicated the way in which the Zeitgeist has been working in the Seventies, with a very definite counter-urbanisation propensity, and a continuing but much more widely dispersed migration into Devon. 'Almost without doubt', Peter Hall wrote in 1980, 'before long a new *Zeigeist* will produce a new vision — or the revival of an old one.'[1] In 1977, in *Europe 2000*[2], he attempted an analysis of the planners duty in relation to changing values. It was a somewhat tall order. 'He must analyse economic, social and cultural history to try to isolate the mainsprings of social change.' Hall argues that the dominant mode of thought in Western Europe has been 'superficially rational' and has been ignoring 'those deeper forces of social change which can cause sudden reversals — in mass values, in the direction of scientific research, in the political agenda — that in a wider historical context can be seen as most important.' He has a suggestion to make on how this insight may be developed. The planner must recognise that history develops by the stimulus of contradictions, must look *not* at trends but at the 'developing counter-eddies under the apparently smooth wave of history'.

Using this technique, and combining it with the evidence of economic dislocation and the impact over the last ten years of such thinkers as Illich, Schumacher and others, Hall suggests that the formative ideas for the future will be first: resource conservation, leading to a decreased preoccupation with consumption of goods but an increased interest in consumption of services; cuts in travel and transportation, accompanied by a wider distribution of small units, the end of giant factory, office or urban complexes; and greatly enhanced use of electronic communication. Secondly, to combat the evident dislike of jobs in mass production industry he envisages an increase in tool-using rather than machine-minding work; and thirdly he expects an emphasis on quality of life, allied with a discriminating use of high technology. Fourthly, he expects the emphasis on small units to find

[1]*Great Planning Disasters*, P. 86.
[2]*Europe 2000*, ed. P. Hall (Duckworth, London, 1977) drew on the work of more than 200 experts in ten different countries over a period of eight years to produce its symposium of prophecies.

political expression, with a reorganisation of social and economic life to decentralise power, with responsibility more widely shared and less scope for bureaucrats or professionals. Many of these ideas are now common currency, and are championed by recognised political parties throughout Europe. The impact has not yet been great, but the French 'green' party picked up four per cent of the vote in the first round of the French presidential election in April 1981, and in July 1982 the West German 'green' party, with nearly eight per cent of the vote, overtook the liberals to become the third largest party in the state.

If these attitudes become more prevalent, the counter-urbanisation trends of the past decade could well become more pronounced. There is, however, a powerful school of thought that regards this spectrum of ideas as maverick, ephemeral, and damaging. Representative of this wholly different approach is the Hudson Report on the UK published three years earlier in 1974, and widely discussed at the time.[1] It analysed in detail the total failure of the UK economy to progress towards the goals of the 1960s, but far from seeing in this the working out of a changing *Zeitgeist*, the report warned of a complacency that failed to recognise the cost of such failure. 'Britain, in a few years, may not be able to afford not only supersonic airplanes, but essential social services, health, education, old age insurance among them — even at present inadequate levels'. It warned of the social, even constitutional disruption that might ensue. 'There is no possibility of supporting Britain's population except through the mechanism of modern industrial society' said the report and called for Britain 'to become a centre for technology and capital-intensive industries'. Dismissing as a 'romantic reaction' the idea that 'no-growth' was an option that could satisfy modern aspirations, the report noted that 'our persistent anxiety over where our civilisation will lead us in the future is justified. . . . But . . . the West is a society which has always furiously expanded, making tools and machines, seeking practical knowledge and wealth . . . it will do Britain no good to deny the nature of its society and culture, and look for sentimental resolutions of a problem which is at the very core of Western civilisation. Britain is a "growth society" by culture.' Certainly the report called for a shift, indeed a 'deep shift', in values, or what it termed 'style', including in the term both psychology and will, in which Britain must overcome its tendency to archaism, its habits of 'conciliation — for its own sake', lack of aggression, deference to what exists, a repeated and characteristic flight into pre-industrial, indeed pre-capitalist fantasies, a suspicion of efficiency as somehow 'common', a dislike for labour itself . . .

In place of what it saw as illusions and evasions, the Hudson Report

[1] James Bellini and others, *The United Kingdom in 1980*, The Hudson Institute, Europe (Associated Business Programmes, 1974). See especially pages 60, 64, 87 and 113.

suggested the revitalisation of the country through an aggressive national development plan, drawing upon an élite of the best brains in the country to form a national planning directorate, a regional planning directorate, and a directorate of science and advanced technology. These brains would analyse society's needs, produce regional and industrial plans and long-range goals for the country as a whole . . . backed by massive investment to 'carry technological innovation to the factory floor'.

Between much in these two approaches there is no necessary economic incompatibility, though there is an obvious political incompatibility between a professional directorate and the sort of decentralised responsibility postulated in *Europe 2000*. It is conceivable that a dynamic national planning directorate might choose to invest in highly decentralised small units and communities, though the resultant choice might call for a very different approach to such matters as education or the shape of human settlements. Nevertheless, in tone and temper the vision of the future embodied in these reports differs fundamentally, both as to what is desirable and as to what is likely to be feasible. The Hudson Report speaks from the world of the Sixties, of the white heat of the technological revolution; *Europe 2000* from the world of the Seventies a world beginning to talk of 'economics as if people mattered' where technology has 'a human face'.[1]

Three years separate the Hudson Report from *Europe 2000* and five years have since gone by. In that time, there has been an intensification of the 'key trend' which *Europe 2000* (page 242) identified, of a deepening international economic crisis impinging on European society in the 1980s and 1990s, with sources of energy and raw materials ever more insecure and manufacuturing less profitable in the face of competition from the newly industrialising countries. Equally, during these years the social tensions and the failure of resources to match aspirations for the social, health and education services have followed the path gloomily predicted for Britain in the Hudson Report. It is impossible, with such highly disparate visions current, to foresee which of the conflicting prescriptions for recovery will win the day, or what will be implied in terms of the dispersal or concentration of population, and the relative attraction of life in rural market towns like Honiton.

If experience suggests that long-range planning is beset by ineluctable ambiguities as to what is probable, feasible, or even desirable, the day-to-day work of environmental control and of statutory provision must still go on. Chapter VII showed how the statutory personal services respond in meeting their obligations. The next chapter pursues the interaction between long-range planning and environmental control at its nexus, the local development plan.

[1]E.F. Schumacher *Small is Beautiful* (Blond and Briggs, London, 1973).

IX

AT GROUND LEVEL

The instrument whereby land for settlement is identified and on which development control decisions are based has been the outline development plan. This is the interpretation at ground level of the settlement pattern postulated by the old County Development and new County Structure Plans.

The plans begin with demographic assumptions. The translation of these statistics into land take-up, however, is tenuous, involving a chain of hypotheses. Just as estimates of future school numbers have to juggle with birthrate projections, and assumptions about the number of school-age children per 10 houses, so the attempt to match residential allocations with demographic projections must make assumptions on the number of houses per acre, and the number of people per house. Industrial allocations require assumptions on the likely age composition of future population, and on the number of industrial jobs per acre, itself dependent on changing assumptions about the likely content of future employment.

Examples of the uncertainties involved may be culled from some of the studies referred to earlier. The Exeter sub-regional study of 1975, for instance, noted that whereas in 1961–66 it appeared that younger people were moving out of the County, by 1966–71 the tendency had apparently ceased, so that it was possible the age balance would be different from, and younger than, earlier studies had suggested. The report made the usual analyses of population, employment, transportation, agriculture, landscape and urban conservation, recreation and tourism, public utilities and 'community support facilities' but inevitably there was no certain way of translating these into foreseeable needs. Notional acreages could be assigned according to the occupancy levels (high for a young population, low for an old), sport and recreational demands, and changing assumptions about the proportion of the population likely to be of working age. The various assumptions considered — of age, of numbers, of housing densities, of types of employment etc. — produced land take-up assessments ranging from 2,000 to 8,400 acres. The figure eventually selected for the published study was 4,450 residential acres plus 820 acres for industrial use.

The preparation of the *Report of Survey* for the Structure Plan, published in 1977, illustrates the problem faced in trying to arrive at a proper allocation of land for the provision of jobs. An analysis was made

81

of employment trends in agriculture, mining and quarrying, manu-facturing, construction and service industries. For the construction and service industries, it was assumed that expansion would occur at the same rate as population expansion; for agriculture, a projection of the 1961–74 trend resulted in employment falling to nil by 1981, an unlikely eventuality, so two assumptions were made instead — that the less steep 1971–74 decline would continue to 1981 and would then halt, giving a higher figure of employment in agriculture in 1991 than the alternative hypothesis, which was that the 1971–74 trend would continue throughout the period under review. For the projection of employment in mining and quarrying the help of the industry was sought, but a comprehensive survey of mineral operators met with a resistance to offer any assurance about employment levels beyond four or five years ahead (to 1981). The expectations about manufacturing prospects were confused by the fact that although in the immediate past jobs in industry had increased in Devon, nationally there had been a decline, with 'competing demands upon a smaller pool of potentially mobile industry'. Furthermore, even if Devon could attract more migrant industry, the tendency in both mining and manufacturing was for increases in productivity to be achieved without a pro-rata increase in the labour force.

These cogitations led to the decision incorporated in the *Draft Written Statement* of the Structure Plan, that although latest population projections for Exeter/East Devon suggested a minimum increase by 1991 of 25,000 and a maximum of 36,000 (only half, as Chapter IV explains, the maximum forecast only three years previously) policy should aim at the lower figure since jobs were unlikely to be forthcoming to sustain the higher. A proviso was included that if immigration seemed to be occurring at the higher level, land would not, after 1981 be made available to permit its continuation; (an unprecedented commitment, since previous documents had never hoped to do more than deflect the inflow). The total land allocation actually tabled, however, matched that used in earlier proposals for housing 52,000 to 64,000 increase.

In other words, the statistical precision is more relaxed than first impressions suggest, and a close examination of Honiton plans bears out this conclusion. For instance Honiton had just (in 1974) had an outline development plan (ODP) and town centre study completed which assumed a probable population of 10,000 in 1991, and allocated 220 acres of residential land and 30 of industrial. The Exeter sub-regional study which looked to 2001 explained various options for settlement in the area, and postulated three possible population figures for Honiton by then, viz: 9,000, 10,000 and 12,000. Though only one of these was larger than Honiton's existing ODP provided for, all were held to warrant an extension of the potentially suitable land so recently indicated for Honiton. For the 9,000, a further 40 acres of industrial land was recommended, with an additional 60 acres for 10,000 and 80 acres for 12,000. These figures may represent changed assumptions, not only about the proportion of the population seeking work, but also about what proportions of the workforce should be employed locally for instance, and how many might commute. The assumptions about extra residential land required are more puzzling however — a further 260 acres for the 9,000 and 310 for the 10,000, both of which had already been catered for in the Honiton plan; and 450 for the 12,000 figure. When the District in March 1978 bought the Army camp and added 30 extra acres to the industrial land, it was agreed with the County that this should be included in the County's total area of land allocated for industry. In the 1974 outline development plan (see Figure 4) 25 acres for industry had been designated beyond the (then) Army camp. The Structure Plan stuck to the carefully-worked out assessment of 30 industrial acres at Honiton, being the 1974 25 plus about five vacant at that time on the old county industrial estate — though in fact double that acreage was by then available.

The relationship between land identified for settlement and future population is, then, much less certain than the apparent statistical precision would suggest. Furthermore, as Chapter IV showed, the attempt to equate population change with any particular time-scale is a very inexact science. (In 1964 for instance, the projected 1981 population for Honiton was 4,800. By 1968 it was 8,000. The actual figure turned out to be 6,500.) The fact that land for development has been identified does not ensure a population increase. The sporadic outbursts of national nomadism that affect the housing market are no doubt profoundly influenced by the vagaries of the economic climate, and the result is a widespread discrepancy between aspiration and actuality. It is a theme which was of some concern to East Devon District Council, contemplating Seaton where the settlement policy had allocated land for a variety of uses in the hope of encouraging growth, but little growth had occurred following the adoption of the policy. Early in 1976 they had minuted that the study of future settlement policy should direct itself to the *means* by which the desired settlement pattern could actually be realised. But if the settlement pattern is based on demographic forecasts that prove false it cannot be realised. The question arises of what useful purpose is served by signifying development land in terms of a particular population at specific dates.

The disadvantages are evident. The false impression is fostered that planners can advise not what may, but what will, have happened to a settlement in ten or fifteen years time; passions are generated over hypotheses that prove to be no more than fantasies; and when population forecasts have to be revised, plans accommodating those population projections cease to be valid. When the options for the

Structure Plan were under discussion, population predictions were undergoing rapid downward revision, and Devon County Council recognised that although outline plans indicated land 'to which there was no fundamental objection to development', there might now be compelling arguments why, in some instance, 'planning permission should not be granted', even before the outline development plans had been amended. East Devon District Council were disturbed to realise that the land estimates for the Structure Plan in some cases *reduced* the area already indicated in agreed ODPs, for some of which, they maintained, public expenditure for infrastructure had already been made or programmed.

According to the evidence of Chapter VII, investment is undertaken by statutory authorities chiefly on the evidence of change actually in progress, coupled with *ad hoc* adaptations to the shifting pressure of unforeseen, unforeseeable and swiftly changing resource availability. With the important exception of sewerage proposals, population forecasts appear to have influenced only two of the decision made for Honiton. The assumption (not now likely to be fulfilled) that 10,000 would be present by 1991 influenced the library service to squeeze an extra 700 square feet on to the site it had acquired for a regional library; and the Education Authority undoubtedly strengthened its case for three separate comprehensive schools by reference to the population projections of the Structure Plan. It is impossible to state whether or not the case would have succeeded at the Department of Education and Science without these projections.

The service most crucially affected by the population forecasts is of course the Water Authority, with its responsibility for sewerage, in the absence of which development cannot proceed. It must be mentioned in passing that here again, the relationship of provision to population totals is only approximate. Chapter V illustrated the changes that have been introduced in the assumptions made at Honiton, with differing allowances made over time for the impact of tourism, or of the level of water consumption or river pollution that different sorts of industry might introduce. Even assumptions about the absorptive capacity of the local river are not immutable, with changing assessments of the prevailing climate and rainfall; and changes in technology at the works can alter the level of pollution passed on to the river.

With its relatively long lead times for the construction of new works, investment decisions by the Water Authorities have to be taken before adequate evidence of the speed and direction of change is available. Because change has been outstripping resource availability, the Authorities have in practice been as much struggling to catch up with the past as to provide for the future. The South West Water Authority, commenting on the various options for the year 2001 proffered in the 1975 *Towards 2001 — The Future of the Exeter Sub-Region* cautioned 'whichever option is finally chosen, a reassessment of all schemes in the sub-Region will have to be made'. An investment by the Authority of something like £1M per year would be needed if the population increase then envisaged were to be adequately serviced. No doubt it was in the light of this and similar comments that the County's Structure Plan Sub-Committee noted in March 1976 'that the Government be urged to assist in the provision of the necessary infrastructure for any development'. But so far from adequate funds being available, in 1980 the Water Authority found itself in its District which included Honiton with some 30 of the 100 treatment works overloaded.

Pressure to catch up with the past may have dominated but has not excluded proposals for the future, for every decision to expand or replace an overloaded works involves working to a new target figure. Certain sizes of sewage works are technically more cost effective than others, which has given sewerage provision a dominant influence in proposing future population targets. Decisions about the future size of Ivybridge, for instance, in South-West Devon, hinged very largely on a sewerage unit capable of serving 8,300 people, and Ivybridge's future was discussed in multiples of that figure, the conclusion recorded in Ivybridge's ODP being to provide for a population of 11,500 by 1991, i.e. one new unit plus the existing works.[1] Although only 5,000 people had settled there by the 1981 census, the sewerage decision will presumably make the larger figure possible. This emphasises the need for development of economically satisfactory smaller-scale units if there is to be a flexible adaptation to changing demographic forecasts, quite apart from the avoidance of the sort of swamping scale of development that has caused so much social distress. Alternatively the Water Authority's present exploration of means whereby developers cover the cost of small-scale extensions may solve the problem.

The sewerage and water authorities thus play an absolutely crucial role in the location of development, and the order in which they tackle their backlog of overloaded works will in effect largely determine where major change can occur. An order of priorities is clearly required, and East Devon District Council raised the point during the discussions in preparation for the Structure Plan about proposals to revise land allocations downwards, when they pleaded that at least the order of priorities implied by existing programmes should be retained. Even this may not prove immutable, for unforeseen attractions — the development of economic opportunities at present unsuspected, or some unheralded metamorphosis of the *Zeitgeist* — may result in the priorities ceasing to reflect current realities. All that can be stressed is the continuing need for the closest liaison between the Water Authorities and those who are monitoring developments to compare them with the

[1]Anne Glyn-Jones, *Village into Town* (University of Exeter and Devon County Council, 1977).

expectations incorporated in the Structure Plan. But the problems raised in Chapter V about the adequacy of resources to service population movement is relevant here. The South West Water Authority's own development plan for 1982 warns that given restrictions on capital expenditure and the need to keep charges to an acceptable level, the priorities for expenditure 'may not necessarily reflect all the priorities for the provision of infrastructure outlined in structure and local plans. The major water services infrastructure requirements identified in the plans could well continue to be the major constraints to new residential and industrial development in the Region'.

Though the land identified for settlement in outline development plans expresses assumptions about expected population on a particular time-scale, the plans neither assure, nor do they necessarily inhibit, development within a particular period. In the 1960s, for instance, when land assigned for housing in the Honiton ODP was used up faster than expected, the processes of amendment were promptly set in train, and an extra 60 acres were added. The real usefulness of the plans has been in the dimension not of time but of space. The indications given in the Honiton ODP of the location where future development would be permitted undoubtedly influenced, in particular, the decisions on siting made by the responsible health and education authorities. Scale was another matter. It suited the Education Authority to come to fairly specific conclusions about numbers, conclusions which may or may not be fulfilled. The Health Authority merely endeavoured to safeguard the possibility of future expansion.

But if specific population targets over specific periods are misleading guides to the determination of settlement land, a basis for development control still has to be applied. Negative guidelines are not hard to identify in the delineation (whether for landscape, mineral, agricultural or other reasons) of areas of restraint, but for over a decade one of the chief concerns of government, enthusiastically abetted by the building industry to the alarm of conservationists, has been the search for green field sites. Local authorities were asked in 1972 (Circular 102/72) to ensure that there was sufficient land with planning permission (or which could readily be granted permission) to sustain private housebuilding for five years, and the requirement was reiterated in Circular 23/81 with its reminder that structure plans should provide a basis for identifying, *inter alia*, a five-year supply of housing land.

Two points arise out of this obligation which the outline development plans endeavour to fulfil. The first is that allocation in an outline development plan does not automatically bring residential land on to the market. A wholly different complex of ideas has been pursued to that end, involving deeply controversial political issues. During the boom period of rapid housing expansion in Honiton in 1968–69 when population was expected to reach 8,000 by 1981, the owners of one particular farm who had been farming the land for half a century and were most reluctant to go were considered to be impeding development, and the County prepared to acquire the land by compulsory purchase for the newly instituted Land Commission under the powers introduced in 1967 by the Labour Government. Before the arrangements were completed, a change of government led to the abolition of the Commission.

The second bears again on the question of timing. The five-year supply assumes a steady progression in the housing market which is not in fact being manifested, but the need remains to identify planning preferences for any particular settlement, whether those selected areas are absorbed in less than, more than, or exactly five years. If outline development plans indicated, within agreed restraints, a hierarchy of zones to which there was no fundamental objection to development the zones could be developed or not as population pressure dictated. Provision already exists for the withholding of planning permission by reason of 'premature development'. This would give the necessary locational guidance to the statutory services without the complication of chimerical and transitory population projections. It is true that this would leave zones low in the hierarchy uncertain of their future. But this is, in reality, the present situation, since areas on the fringe of existing ODPs may find themselves included in a revision, and areas within may never be required, or may (as reassessments for the Structure Plan suggested) find themselves outside a redrawn boundary.

When structure planning replaced the old county development plans, statutory provision was made for the framing of local plans (though the plans themselves will, like the old outline development plans, not require ministerial approval) to give land-use expression to the demographic and economic objectives promulgated in the structure plan. In August 1981, however, Department of the Environment circular 23/81 requested planning authorities to consult their DOE regional office to establish whether there was a clear need for the particular statutory local plan, and to satisfy the Department that work on the plan was realistic and would result in the plan being on deposit within a year for objections to be registered. Such plans would not be needed where the structure plan provided an adequate framework, nor where little or no development pressure was expected. Thus they would seldom be needed for a village or small town where little change was expected. The absence of such a local plan would not in itself be sufficient reason for refusing a planning application. Where local plans were needed, their purpose would be to provide locations for the future supply of land for housing and industry, to define the precise boundaries of areas of restraint, or to co-ordinate programmes for development. It is expected that eventually the Honiton ODP will be replaced by a statutory local plan.

To this somewhat cool appraisal of the necessity for the production of labour-intensive detailed local plans may be added the indication — admittedly tentative on such a narrow geographical foundation — that the use of local plans to signify the proposals of the statutory services has proved so ephemeral that these land reservations on an ODP can soon become inappropriate, and must be either ignored or officially amended. Chapter VII illustrated some of the reasons that compel the readjustment of intentions with regard to the use of land by the statutory services. The reservation of sites in the outline development plan theoretically safeguarded them against development for other purposes, but in most cases they were in any case safeguarded by the fact that they were in public ownership. In the case of the main exception, the old people's home site in Dowell Street, the sterilisation of alternative development led to pressure being exerted — and acceded to — to dispense with the plan designation.

But if the potential of ODPs to interpret long-range plans, or to illustrate how the delivery of statutory services is being coordinated, has been over-rated, there remains another aspect of planning at ground level, one with which the earliest planning legislation was chiefly concerned, and which some would still regard as the central task of planning — the creation of a worth-while physical environment. 'The planning machinery exists primarily to put into practice ideas for improvement of the surroundings' stated the County Planning Officer for East Sussex, Andrew Thorburn, 1982 president of the Royal Town Planning Institute, in an address to the Conservation Society's AGM at Reading in 1978, and a somewhat similar if perhaps more partisan approach seems to lie behind the definition of planning propounded in the Manifesto of the West Midlands Labour Party: 'planning was instituted to protect the community from unscrupulous land-owners and developers'. Implicit in these quotations are the two sides of the coin of environmental improvement — conservation on the one hand and the instigation or at least regulation of change on the other. Much of the dismay over development in past decades has centred not only on the social consequences where established communities are destroyed by 'swamping', but also on the quality of design of buildings and the layout of estates. The Devon Conservation Forum's 1976 analysis, *Urbanisation in Devon*, referred specifically to the poor quality of much of the building that covered some 20,000 acres ('much of it good farm land') built over since the war. They drew attention to examples of developments in Devon which they considered had been conspicuously successful[1] but, in accepting the need for some new building, they

[1]Others have since attracted approbation at national level. Shilhay in Exeter, for instance, won the Department of the Environment/RIBA Good Design in Housing Award in 1979.

objected to 'large tracts of homogenous housing, with their monotonous layout and repetitive design'. They complained of imported and alien materials and insensitive street furniture and lighting — very much the minutiae of planning, but details making an immediate impact on the physical environment. It seems possible that the almost Pavlovian opposition that so often greets proposals for rural development may owe a good deal to dislike of its aesthetic quality. Few British people seem to regard chalets as desecrating the Alps.

Honiton's first ODP, in addition to recording the relevant areas of great landscape value and outstanding natural beauty designated on the County Map, showed listed buildings and expressed the Authority's intention to designate a Conservation Area under the newly-passed Civic Amenities Act of 1967; an intention emphasized by the inclusion of Honiton as a town of 'special character' in the 1969 second review of the County Development Plan. The Borough Council, for reasons which are not clear, had not been co-operative, maintaining that since most of the buildings in the area concerned (the picturesque main street) were listed anyway, there was no point, and they preferred to await the full town centre study which, it was intended, should accompany a planned revision of the outline development plan. The County's anxiety was due to the fact that although there were indeed some 87 protected buildings or groups of buildings, the complex of which they formed part could be damaged by unsympathetic treatment of unlisted buildings among them. After about nine months of controversy the County decided to defer to the Borough's opinion. However the Conservation Area was duly incorporated in the 1974 Town Centre Study (see Figure 5), was accepted by all concerned and duly designated by the County early in 1974.

The Town Centre Study, going into much more detail than is covered by the simple ODP, concentrated not merely on architecture but also on the whole relationship between urban layout and the provision of a satisfactory environment, looking for instance at the direction of traffic flows and the location of shops as well as at the quality of buildings. To improve the shopping area, which was found to be very elongated, it was proposed that permissions for retail use should not be extended along the High Street, and the area accepted for retail use should be improved by attempting to provide rear access for deliveries; by trying to deflect trunk road traffic coming from the Axminster direction north-east to the bypass link even when its destination was south-west, and thus more directly reached by going through the town; by 'traffic management' and the provision of more car parks so as to remove vehicles from the main shopping street. There were also many proposals for environmental improvement, including pedestrianisation schemes, landscaping, tree planting, a riverside walkway and land-scaped amenity area. In particular, three areas of the town were singled

89

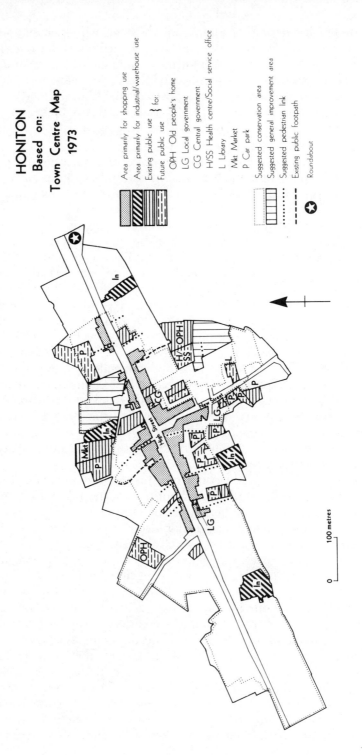

HONITON
Based on:
Town Centre Map
1973

Area primarily for shopping use
Area primarily for industrial/warehouse use
Existing public use } for:
Future public use

OPH Old people's home
LG Local government
CG Central government
H/SS Health centre/Social service office
L Library
Mkt Market
P Car park

Suggested conservation area
Suggested general improvement area
Suggested pedestrian link
Existing public footpath
Roundabout

0   100 metres

Fig. 5   Honiton Town Centre Proposals 1974

90

out as suitable for 'the comprehensive application of improvement grants,' with the further recommendation that two General Improvement Areas under the Housing Act 1969 be declared, 'where more fundamental improvements to the fabric and lay-out are envisaged' and within which 'improvements to the general environment as well as to individual buildings may be made, in certain instances with the aid of grants from the Department of the Environment.' Sites were earmarked for the expressed needs of the various statutory authorities (see Figure 5).

So far as the implementation of the recommendations was concerned, the study considered that, with certain specific exceptions, it was 'desirable and possible for the items contained in the summary of town centre proposals and policies to be put into effect by 1981'. Appendix 8 lists the twenty-odd proposals made and shows the extent to which they have been implemented. The Conservation Area was designated, a new roundabout was put at the top end of the town, and a pedestrian way through to the High Street was included in a new housing development. The library, already under construction when the plan was published, has been opened. The other suggestions, however, have fallen by the wayside. A number of improvement grants have been made to individual property owners in various parts of Honiton, including those mentioned in the Plan, but no General Improvement Areas have been declared, and thus enhanced environmental improvement grants have not been payable.

The fact that other proposals have not been implemented is probably no more than a reflection of the usual difficulty in matching resources with chronology. Inevitably this must limit the hopes for constructing attractive town centres. In this connection, it is significant that although the study envisaged a future population of 10,000, there is no provision for any civic or social focal point. Money was as usual at the root of the problem. A Tenants Association had been suggesting, back in 1965, that if Honiton was to grow there ought to be a good town hall, with a hall that could be booked. The old Borough Council had reserved a site for such a purpose, but the (then) Ministry of Housing and Local Government had refused loan sanction. In early 1968 with the feasibility study nearing completion, the Borough Council had contemplated seeking land for 'a real town hall or civic centre', with assembly rooms, kitchens, car parks, council chamber and committee rooms, and perhaps offering accommodation to such county or national government undertakings as needed local offices. A 'Civic Buildings Committee' again approached the Ministry, only to be told in June 1969 that 'at the present time there is no prospect of obtaining loan sanction for new civic buildings'. The Honiton ODP and Town Centre Study was prepared at a time of special difficulty, with reorganisation pending, and it was said of public buildings, that 'in view of the present

91

St John's Close, proposed General Improvement Area   Andrew Teed

uncertainties concerning the size and location of local government administrative centres, no additional allocation is made for such uses. Should it prove necessary, however, any proposal in this respect will be considered on its merits in the light of the present report, as will any other proposal for accommodating public uses.' Before its disappearance the Borough Council had entered into negotiations with the trustees of a centre-town hall, and this the Council arranged to lease with the designation 'Town Hall'. A site was also ear-marked by the swimming pool on the edge of the existing town for what the study called a 'multi-purpose building for entertainment and other public activities', and here the new District Council has developed a sports hall.

It is disappointing to record that no progress has been made on such modest proposals for ameliorating the local environment as a riverside walk and the planting of mature trees in the High Street. A specific built-up area like a small town is the least speculative level at which planning operates, where integrated proposals could surely hope to bear fruit. If local authorities lack the funds, one might have hoped for local voluntary initiatives, and one cannot help but wonder whether the energies of local leaders have been absorbed in the more abstruse and academic aspects of the planning process to the detriment of the local scene.

X

CONCLUSIONS

The political, administrative and research effort involved in planning over the 15 years of this study has been prodigious; moreover, the detail and complexity of the documents have tended to increase over time, with the analyses or reports of survey, for instance, lengthening from 96 pages in 1964 via 119 pages in 1969 to 184 by 1979. Appendix 9 lists the various plans, surveys and studies bearing on Honiton between 1964 and 1979 — the period of this study and also, coincidentally, almost exactly the lifetime of the regional economic planning boards. Appendix 10 gives an indication of the ground they covered and of the extent of consultation and liaison required to produce them. Councillors charged with making decisions in the planning field have, over the period, had to assimilate 16 publications incorporating over 1,700 pages of information, nearly 600 statistical tables, 136 graphs and diagrams; and study over 100 maps.

At county council level, many committees have been involved. The AIC, SWEPC and feasibility studies, for instance, impinged on the responsibilities of, and were dissected and debated in, the Industrial Development Sub-Committee (later the Industry and Tourism Sub-Committee), the County Map Sub-Committee, the County Planning Committee, the Legal and General Purposes Committee, the Chairmen and Special Purposes Committee and the Finance Committee, as well of course as at the County Council itself.

Thus the planning process itself involves a considerable commitment of time, money and expertise. Comprehensive statutory planning is still not 40 years old, and all those involved have been learning by trial and error as decade succeeds decade. This chapter seeks to summarise what it was endeavouring to do, as exemplified at Honiton; what it succeeded in doing; and what inherent limitations impeded its success.

The Introduction identified three strands in the planning process with which this analysis is particularly concerned: management of the delivery of statutory services; the identification and pursuit of social and economic, i.e. political, objectives; and the immediate task of 'town and country planning', exercising control over land use and the physical environment.

Clearly the statutory powers of development control have had their influence on the way Honiton has developed. There has been no sprawl across the bypass, the old and attractive main street is protected, and

94

the statutory services have been forewarned of the location, if not the timing, of new building. So far as the management function is concerned, where statutory provision has failed, as in the case of the 'sewage embargo' (though as Chapter V explained, this is not the main reason for the cessation of house-building), the inadequacy has been due not to lack of foresight or intent but to lack of resources. By considering all Devon settlements together in one document, the old County Development Plans and the new Structure Plan have focused the attention of investors, both public and private, and provided a point of departure for liaison. In practice, the response has been largely incremental. The real goad to action has been not so much the long-term policies or projections of the Plan as the actual experience of development pressure, as evidenced by planning applications. This market pressure is of course not geographically free but is channelled according to the residential areas indicated by the local land-use plans — but these plans, in their turn, are redrawn in the light of development pressures.

In effect, then, it is the prospects for the next five years that are influencing the investment decisions of the statutory services. The plans, however, cover 15 year periods. It is taken for granted that the latter part of the period will be subject to revision in the light of events, but if the revision is very extensive it calls into question the value of making detailed assessments and proposals for the later dates. The two variables of demographic changes and available resources have differed from the assumptions made sufficiently to constitute just such grounds for doubt; and while it is true that there remain some optimists who believe that future levels of prosperity can be not only planned for but also achieved, even they are less sanguine about influencing the numbers of people or where they will live and work. The Planning Advisory Group in 1965 criticised the old county development plans for their rigidity in the face of changing circumstances; and in their proposals for structure planning, endeavoured to separate the strategic from the more transitory aspects of planning. This survey suggests that uncertainty has penetrated the strategic levels to an extent unimagined in the more confident days of the Sixties.

The pursuit of social and economic goals attracts additional inconstancies. Chapter VIII drew attention to the volatility of values, and to changes, even where objectives remain constant, in the received wisdom as to how the objectives may be best pursued — whether, for instance, economic growth and the maximising of employment opportunities could best be achieved by concentrating or by dispersing sites for industry.

There is a further problem which has only been touched on by implication so far, and that is the gap between what is actually happening, and what is known about it, with the result that out-of-date assumptions are fed into the system. An obvious recent example is the belief manifested in documents of the Seventies that rural areas were steadily depopulating. It is evident from the 1981 census that this is at present substantially untrue, though no comprehensive analysis is yet available of the age groups involved. A similar time-lag undermined the studies of the Sixties recommending and exploring the feasibility of town development schemes. The AIC and SWEPC recommendations were not, it is true, greeted with enthusiasm at the political level in Devon, but even in the case of Honiton, the one town anxious to co-operate, the proposal was nullified by events, for no metropolitan area any longer had people to export.

The collection of up-to-date data, apart from its expense and its theological dangers (Yahweh, after all, forbade the numbering of the people), is frequently resented by the general public, particularly by the business community whose attitude to the filling up of government forms is well known. The fact remains that current decisions are more influenced by what are thought to be current realities than by 15-, 20-, or 40-year prognostications, and monitoring the current situation is probably a more essential activity than futurology.

The more permanent features of the environment, both natural and man-made, have by now been tabulated in the course of the surveys since 1974 preceding the development plans. The contemporary up-dating of inventories is concerned with land use changes, and with such other human activities as the formation of families or the opening of shops ·and businesses. No matter how much data is amassed, the making of every decision seems to demand more; and furthermore, there is always the danger, as every researcher knows, that the more data are collected, the more tempting it becomes to explore yet more areas of ignorance, forgetting that in the public service information is only worth collecting if it is useful as well as interesting. Not all reports referred to in this study have steered clear of the temptation. The spread of micro-electronics enhances the danger, for while one might hope that the rapid collation and retrieval of data might make accurate information more swiftly accessible, there is the risk of computers disgorging kilometres of indigestible print-outs. Hard-headed discretion is required, both in the collection and in the processing of data.

The Conservative Government which came to power in 1979, unlike its predecessor of 1970–74, displayed a marked disenchantment with the edifice of economic planning constructed over the previous decades, and in August 1979 the regional economic planning boards were abolished.[1] Though firmly committed to environmental planning, the

[1] A minor but practically significant consequence was that since Devon County Council had based its statistical analyses for the Structure Plan on the SWEPC geographical units, the Economic Planning Areas which did not correspond to local government and OPCS usage, the abolition of SWEPC is likely to deprive future statistics of ready comparability over time — one of the *sine qua non* of assessing trends.

new Government expressed considerable dissatisfaction with the manner in which it was being carried out. In 1980 the Local Governent Planning and Land Act introduced simplifications in the process of making, altering, repealing or replacing structure plans. Department of the Environment Circular 23/81 of August 1981 set out to elucidate further simplifications 'designed to reduce costs and manpower' and 'enable overall savings to be made'. Experience had shown, said the circular, that both in local and central government it had been all too easy to lose clarity, conciseness, and above all, time. Future work must be limited to essentials, the plan to consist simply of policies and general proposals with an accompanying explanatory memorandum. Past surveys had been over-elaborate, and new survey work was to be kept to the minimum necessary. The circular firmly distinguished the inventory aspect of planning from the controversial aspect, i.e. policy intentions; no longer was there any requirement to prepare a report of the results of review work or to publicise it.

The DOE circular also restricted the exercises in public participation. Public consultation over both the fashioning of local plans and the altering of structure plans was in future to be limited to six weeks.

Since 1968 public participation has been a statutory requirement. Following the publication of the Exeter sub-regional study, which was launched at a press conference in October 1975, public meetings were arranged throughout the study area, publicity for which was made available in libraries and through newspaper advertisements. Copies of the report were deposited in libraries, and sent to all district councils concerned, as well as to statutory undertakings, MPs and county councillors. All town and parish councils in the area were asked for their views. Nearly 1,500 copies of the report were made available. But the six public meetings held (four in Exeter, one in Honiton and one in Tiverton), drew a total attendance of only 287 people, over a third of whom were from parish councils.

While the Exeter sub-region were concentrating on their immediate prospects, a county-wide preliminary exercise in public participation for the Structure Plan had been in progress. Seven key issues were selected by the County (later amended to eight by the addition of agriculture and forestry), covering settlements (scale, facilities etc.); employment; shops; transport; recreation and tourism; minerals; and conservation. Their opinion of the relative importance of these topics was canvassed from district, town and parish councils, assorted nationalised industries and other bodies such as the National Trust and the Forestry Commission. Some 28,000 questionnaires were distributed, in addition to cut-out questionnaires in half-page advertisements in every Devon newspaper. Publicity was sought via TV and radio announcements, articles in the press, and posters on public display in libraries, health centres, and district and parish offices. As a result, 1,617 individual forms were returned in addition to replies from 11 associations, amenity societies and pressure groups. The Devon Branch of the Conservation Society distributed 3,400 copies of its own questionnaire through Women's Institutes, Exeter Library and via letters to the press, and received 530 completed forms.

The participation exercise ensured that the contents of the draft plan were widely known. But although the quality and extent of the response may well have been adequate to provide Devon County Council with the guidance it sought on what matters were of most concern to the public, it cannot be claimed that this was a very intense level of public participation in a county of nearly a million inhabitants. Perhaps the issues were too complex, the documents too intimidating, though the County did its best with pamphlets and posters to simplify and pinpoint the main topics for discussion. When the Skeffington Report of 1969 drew attention to the importance of public participation in planning, it appeared to be much more concerned with the local environment than with the more abstruse socio-economic parameters of 'structure' planning. The prospects for manipulating tomorrow's world are of intrinsic interest to some casts of mind, but the point at which most people's interest engages is at a far more parochial level: where will the double yellow lines go? Which trees are going to come down? Is there going to be a youth club? If I start a business in my garage, shall I be told to stop? Are they going to build on the allotments? If the resolution of such issues seems to fall rather far short of the Utopian hopes that fire the imagination of the young enthusiast for planning, it may nevertheless be the level at which more can be achieved towards the construction of New Jerusalem than by all the participatory exercises in county, region or nationwide futurology which have so preoccupied politicians, planners and people over the last 20 years. If the emphasis in rural planning is indeed shifting, as Professor Cherry for instance detects,[1] from the county strategic view to 'forms of rural management at local scale', there may well be an improved level of local involvement.

The setting of social and economic goals is part of the daily business of modern government and of the democratic political process; and statutory planning is expected to incorporate the guidance the goals suggest. The Secretary of State's examination of the Devon Structure Plan resulted in some re-wording of proposals where it was thought that such national objectives as the safeguarding of agricultural land or of protected landscapes were insufficiently strongly expressed. But as this study indicates, there are limits to the extent to which the identification of goals at macro level can be translated into practical proposals at micro level; or, to borrow Faludi's terminology,[2] the extent to which

[1] *Town and Country Planning Journal*, October 1982, p. 243.
[2] A. Faludi, *Planning Theory*, Pergamon Press, 1973.

98

normative and functional planning can be induced to coincide. Moreover, attempts at co-ordination are made more difficult by the increase in the rate of change. When the *Draft Written Statement* of the Structure Plan was circulated in 1977 for instance, SWEPC commented that 'with national economic recovery, there will be opportunities for faster economic growth in Devon than now foreseen. The Planning Council therefore urge that the Devon Structure Plan should place particular emphasis on the claims of the Plymouth area . . .' The Plan was amended by the addition of residential and industrial acres in the Plymouth area. There is still time for this forecast to prove true, but the period between the circulation of the draft and the publication of the plan as finally approved registered only declining prosperity — so much so that many road proposals entered as policy in the earlier versions had been expunged by the time the approved version appeared. The successive versions illustrate, too, the speed with which policies were being re-assessed to accommodate changing viewpoints — mention has already been made (see above page 76) of the revised attitudes towards permitting the development of homes and jobs in the countryside.

At the practical level, the attempts to add, from choice, management of the local economy to the statutory duties under the Town and Country Planning Acts appear to have had limited effect. Social and economic changes have indeed occurred — in Honiton population has increased markedly and new businesses have been established. But, as Chapter VI shows, the dynamic has been people pursuing what they saw as in their own interests — in conformity with the planning system, which has guided the areas of settlement, but not particularly closely in accordance with its expectations.

The relationship between policy formulation and subsequent achievement has proved tenuous, nor has it been possible to combine political objectives, management of the various public services, and environmental control into the comprehensive planned whole that seemed so attractive a prospect in earlier decades. The extent of current unemployment is encouraging some local authorities to involve their planning departments directly in entrepreneurial ventures for which they may or may not have the requisite expertise, and whose effectiveness will no doubt become the subject of much future cost/benefit analysis. But here too there remain evident limits, not least those of obtaining investment resources, to what government, whether national or local, can achieve. The Britain of the Eighties and Nineties will be shaped as much by the perceptions — and resulting responses — of individuals as by the decision of the governments they elect. Insofar as the statutory planning process charts contemporary developments and articulates future options, it contributes, though not uniquely, to the increase of awareness on which those perceptions are based. Books, newspapers, and TV and radio programmes are also exploring the contemporary scene and probing the future. A subtle interaction is occurring in which experience and analysis combine to heighten awareness and alter attitudes. And it is this interaction which is determining the actualities of change.

HONITON POPULATION 1801–1981

	Military	RG's Civilian Estimate to 1973. Devon County Council after 1974	RG's Estimate of "Home" Pop.	Census
1801				2377
1811				2735
1861				3301
1871				3464
1881				3358
1891				3216
1901				3271
1911				3191
1921				3093
1931				3008
1951	1103[1]			**4613**
1961	801			**4718**
1962	487	4098		
1963	506	4175		
1964	–	4210		
1965	54	4320		
1966	699	4410	5130	
1967	659	4598	5270	
1968	646	5143	5800	
1969	?	5411		
1970	631	5451	6080	
1971	–		5320	**5072**
1972	–			
1973	–	5809[2]		
1974	–			
1975	–			
1976	–	5260		
1977	–	5925		
1978	–	6220		
1979	–	6390		
1980	–	6515		
1981	–			**6547**

[1] May 1950 figure – 1951 not available.
[2] Probably due to the temporary influx of Uganda Asians.

APPENDIX 2

POPULATION ANALYSIS BY AGE: HONITON, AXMINSTER AND GB, 1961 to 1981

		1961 Total	%	1971 Total	%	1981† Total	%	Per cent Change Since 1971
Honiton MB	0–15	1000	25.5	1240	24.4	1395	21.5	+12.5
	16–44	1260*	32.2	1715	33.8	2371	36.5	+38.3
	45–59F/64M	901	23.0	1050	20.7	1149	17.7	+9.4
	60+F/65+M	756	19.3	1070	21.1	1577	24.3	+47.4
		3917*	100	5075	100	6492	100	+27.9
Honiton RD	0–15	1742	24.7	1840	23.8	1973	23.2	+7.2
	16–44	2390	33.8	2590	33.4	3243	38.0	+25.2
	45–59F/64M	1650	23.4	1630	21.0	1594	18.7	-2.2
	60+F/65+M	1277	18.1	1690	21.8	1716	20.1	+1.5
		7059	100	7750	100	8526	100	+10.0
Axminster RD	0–15	3156	21.9	3100	20.2	2658	17.3	-14.3
	16–44	4528	31.4	4365	28.5	4613	30.0	+5.7
	45–59F/64M	3556	24.7	3655	23.9	3231	21.0	-11.6
	60+F/65+M	3167	22.0	4205	27.4	4880	31.7	+16.1
		14407	100	15325	100	15382	100	+0.4
Great Britain (In Thousands)	0–15	12647	24.7	13684	25.4	11940	22.3	-12.7
	16–44	19499	38.0	20087	37.2	21631	40.4	+7.7
	45–59F/64M	11584	22.6	11397	21.1	10527	19.6	-7.6
	60+F/56+M	7554	14.7	8810	16.3	9459	17.7	+7.4
		51284	100	53978	100	53557	100	-0.8

*Census figures adjusted by subtraction of troops at Army Camp.

†Resident on census night. Non-resident figures by age not yet available.

UNEMPLOYMENT IN HONITON EMPLOYMENT EXCHANGE AREA, INCLUDING SIDMOUTH AND OTTERY ST MARY, COMPARED WITH THE AVERAGE FOR DEVON, THE SOUTH WEST, ENGLAND AND THE UK

	Honiton EEA	Devon	SW	Eng.	UK
1964	1.5	2.3	1.5	1.3	1.7
1965	1.9	2.4	1.5	1.1	1.5
1966	2.4	2.4	1.7	1.2	1.5
1967	3.4	3.2	2.5	2.0	2.3
1968	4.9	3.3	2.5	2.1	2.5
1969	5.0	3.6	2.6	2.1	2.4
1970	5.4	3.7	2.8	2.3	2.6
1971	5.4	4.6	3.3	3.0	3.5
1972	5.7	4.3	3.4	3.3	3.8
1973	4.7	3.1	2.4	2.4	2.7
1974	4.7	3.4*	2.6	2.4	2.6
1975	6.4	5.9	4.7	3.9	4.1
1976	7.9	7.6	6.3	5.3	5.7
1977	8.8	8.7	6.8	5.7	6.2
1978	8.2	8.2	6.5	5.6	6.1
1979	7.6	7.4	5.7	5.2	5.8
1980	7.8	8.5	6.7	6.8	7.4
1981	10.6	12.0	10.0	NA	11.4

*New County

These percentages are based on the estimated total number of employees plus those seeking work. (The self-employed are not included in that total.) There have been changes during the period in the methods of estimating total numbers, and in 1974 the numbers unemployed were also, in certain months and areas, an estimate, due to "industrial action" at some offices of the Employment Services Agency. Present proportions are based on confidential returns sought annually from firms employing five or more, and sought triennially from those with less than five employees.

Sources: Annual Abstract of Statistics and Manpower Services Commission (Regional Manpower Intelligence Unit, Bristol).

HONITON HOUSING COMPLETIONS 1960–81

Year ending June	Private	Local Authority	Total
1960–61	6	40	46
1961–62	9	–	9
1962–63	11	32	43
1963–64	5	–	5
1964–65	13	8	21
1965–66	31	44	75
1966–67	69	22	91
1967–68	185	107	292
1968–69	68	–	68
1969–70	12	–	12
1970–71	8	28	36
1971–72	43	–	43
1972–73	36	–	36
1973–74	20	9	29
1974–75 ′	35	15	50
1975 last 6 months	2	–	2
Calendar Year			
1976	–	6	6
1977	161	–	161[†]
1978	93	–	93
1979	65	–	65
1980	34	17*	51
1981	13	–	13

Source: DCC Central Intelligence Services.

*Plus two army huts temporarily converted for emergency use.
[†] Some of these were almost certainly completed in 1976.

BUSINESSES IN HONITON CLASSIFIED BY 1980 SICs

		1964	1971	1980
Division 0	Agriculture, Forestry, Fishing	3	3	5
Division 1	Energy and Water Supply	3	0	0
Division 2	Manufacturers: Metals, Mineral Products, Chemicals	3	3	3
Division 3	Metal Goods and Engineering	4	5	12
Division 4	Other Manufacturing	9	13	14
Division 5	Construction	18	29	30
Division 6	Distribution and Repairs	67	87*	99
Division 6.6	Hotels and Catering	26	25	22
Division 7	Transport and Communications	5	10	12
Division 8	Business Services	17	24	27
Division 9	Other Services	11	14	18
		166	213	242

Source: Yellow Pages, advertisements in local brochures.

Excluded: Farmers and growers, old people's homes, doctors, nurses, chiropodists, vets.

* For purposes of comparison, Devon County Council's *Honiton Report* of 1973 found "some 90" shops in 1971.

PERCENTAGES BY AGE GROUP OF UNEMPLOYED REGISTERED AT
HONITON AND SIDMOUTH OFFICES OF HONITON EMPLOYMENT
EXCHANGE AREA 1974–1981

Males	"a" Under 54		"b" 55–59		"c" 60+		b + c	
	Hon.	Sid.	Hon.	Sid.	Hon.	Sid.	Hon.	Sid.
July 1974	25.2	18.2	10.9	12.1	63.9	69.7	74.8	81.8
July 1975	68.7	44.8	4.5	12.5	26.7	42.7	31.2	55.2
Jan 1976	58.5	55.2	10.8	9.8	30.7	35.0	41.5	44.8
July 1976	51.4	39.3	10.3	16.1	38.3	44.6	48.6	60.7
Jan 1977	60.1	46.2	9.0	13.8	30.9	40.0	39.9	53.8
July 1977	59.4	39.7	7.7	13.7	32.9	46.6	40.6	60.3
Jan 1978	60.6	45.6	8.6	12.5	30.8	41.9	39.4	54.4
July 1978	53.5	33.3	12.8	16.1	33.7	50.6	46.5	66.7
Jan 1979	55.3	45.8	11.3	13.4	33.4	40.8	44.7	54.2
July 1979	50.0	31.2	13.9	13.1	36.1	55.7	50.0	68.8
Jan 1980	50.6	44.1	16.9	14.5	32.5	41.4	49.4	55.9
July 1980	51.4	45.4	16.2	20.7	32.4	33.9	48.6	54.6
Jan 1981	61.5	53.6	15.5	16.1	23.0	30.3	38.5	46.4
July 1981	59.1	47.7	14.3	17.1	26.6	35.2	40.9	52.3

Females	Under 54		55+	
July 1974	64.0	69.2	36.0	30.8
July 1975	88.1	86.8	11.9	13.2
Jan 1976	90.5	90.0	9.5	10.0
July 1976	91.0	72.7	9.0	27.3
Jan 1977	87.8	95.4	12.2	4.6
July 1977	96.6	90.6	3.4	9.4
Jan 1978	92.6	84.7	7.4	15.3
July 1978	91.7	75.7	8.3	24.3
Jan 1979	88.9	87.1	11.1	12.9
July 1979	87.6	82.9	12.4	17.1
Jan 1980	88.8	82.5	11.2	17.5
July 1980	85.7	71.9	14.3	28.1
Jan 1981	86.2	86.3	13.8	13.7
July 1981	91.2	86.5	8.8	13.5

Source: Honiton Job Centre. The totals on which this breakdown is based run lower than
the figures given in Appendix 3 because they exclude registrations with Careers Offices,
and also, since January 1977, the Professional and Executive Register. The CO and
PER records do not permit the degree of disaggregation required for this table. It may
be presumed that the CO register is mostly young; and also that 'early retireds' are quite
likely to be on the PER register. In July, but not in January, the CO register tends to
exceed considerably the PER register. The bias of elderly remains true but is probably
exaggerated in this table especially in July.

HONITON HOUSING FORECASTS 1977–1986

as supplied to Devon County Council by East Devon District Council

Date of Forecast	1977 P	1977 LA	1978 P	1978 LA	1979 P	1979 LA	1980 P	1980 LA	1981 P	1981 LA	1982 P	1982 LA	1983 P	1983 LA	1984 P	1984 LA	1985 P	1985 LA	1986 P	1986 LA
1976	51	8	61	18	35	30	37	—	34	—	22	—	120	—						
1977			50	18	29	—	38	—	38	—	130	—	140	—						
1978					70	—	119	43	105	—	140	—	120	—						
1979							30	17	125	26	134	—	80	16						
1980									58	—	61	—			65	—	65	—		
1981															111	—	85	16	50	0

P = Private
LA = Local Authority

107

TOWN CENTRE PROPOSALS

In the *Honiton Report* by Devon County Council and Honiton
Borough Council 1974

Parking	*Action Taken by 1981?*
1973–81 Construct 3 new car parks in King St	No
1981–91 New car park in Clapper Lane	No
Small roundabout at High St/Kings Road Junction	Yes
Incorporation of New St in King St servicing loop (dependent on construction of new distributor road not expected to be complete by 1981)	No
Improvements between Clapper Lane proposed car park and High St	No

Rear Access Servicing Roads	
North West High St – Service Link from George St	No
South West High St (in conjunction with King St car parks)	No
South East High St	New road constructed to new houses, but too far from back of shops for use in servicing
North East High St (in conjunction with Clapper Lane car park)	No

Pedestrian Ways	
Link from Manor Place	No
Link from Orchard Way	Yes
Link from King St Existing private paths in use	No change
Link from Clapper Lane Car Park	No
Conservation area designated	Yes
Walkway by River Gissage	No

Parking	Action Taken by 1981?
Landscaped amenity area at Ottery Moore Lane	No
Planting of semi-mature trees in High St	No
Landscaping of present and proposed car parks	No
General Improvement Areas (Landscaping, provision of garages, some demolition):	Not declared
Newlands/Silver St/St Johns Close	
East Queen St	
Site allocated for Health Centre and Social Services	Not used (Medical Centre added at Hospital)
Site allocated for new Library	Yes
Site allocated for Old People's Home	Not used

PLANS AND PLANNING STUDIES INCORPORATING
HONITON SINCE 1964

Apart from the various annual programmes framed by the providers of public services to which occasional reference has been made in the text, there have over the 15 years covered by this report been 16 planning documents affecting Honiton, many of them involving all three planning strands examined in this report, namely political aims, management of services and the methodology of environmental change. The documents are listed below in chronological order, together with a code expressing their origin and purpose; and their scope in relation to the then current administrative responsibilities, bearing in mind that prior to 1974 Plymouth and Exeter were County Boroughs for whose planning the Administrative County was not responsible. As the introduction explained, County Development Plans stemming from the 1947 Town and Country Planning Act were primarily concerned with land use. They consisted of a statement of policies and maps on an ordnance base and excluded generally the social and economic aims on which they were based. The Structure Plan, made in response to the 1971 Act, was required to consist of a statement of policies and diagrams (not on an ordnance base), and to be explicit about the social and economic assumptions and objectives of the Plan.

Origin The documents originate from three sources: central government: CG; local government: LG; and consultants to local government: C; the two central government documents were prepared for SWEPC by the civil service. The consultants' report was by Associated Industrial Consultants at the behest of Plymouth County Borough and the old Devon Administrative County. The remaining 13 documents were prepared by Devon County Planning Department, one of them in conjunction with Exeter County Borough planning department.

Purpose Five documents shown in bold type in the table below expressed the result of political decisions – P1; eleven were compiled as aids to the making of decisions – P2. of the five expressing decisions, two referred exclusively to Honiton, namely the two non-statutory outline development plans. The other three were statutory documents dealing with the whole area for which the Devon Planning Authority was currently responsible).

Scope Four levels are involved:
1 Honiton itself: H1; there are three documents in this category, all of which come from the period 1968–74. Any up-dating of the local development plans will be the responsibility of the East Devon District Council, established in 1974.
2 Honiton plus adjacent areas which were also the responsibility of Devon County Council as the Local Planning Authority: H2.
3 Honiton within the context of the whole area for which Devon County Council was responsible: H3. Of these eight documents, four date from before local government reorganisation and apply to the old Administrative County. Four refer to the post-1974 County incorporating the old County Boroughs.
4 Honiton within the context of areas exceeding those for which the County was responsible: H4. These four documents, two referring to the South West as a whole and two combining all or part of the Administrative County with old County Boroughs, all date from 1966–1974, before reorganisation.

PLANS AND PLANNING STUDIES INCORPORATING HONITON, SINCE 1964

Year	Title	Classification	Pages	Tables	Graphs & Diagrams	Maps	Copies printed
1964	County Development Plan First Review						
	Analysis of Survey	LG/P2/H3	96	48	6	10 +9 supplied separately	
	Written Statement	LG/P1 H3	56	13			
1966	AIC Report *Industry & Growth*	C/P2/H4	107	42	23	3	
1967	SWEPC *Region with a Future*	CG/P2/H4	154	59			
1968	**Honiton Outline Development Plan**	LG/P1/H1	1			1	
1968	Honiton Feasibility Study	LG/P2/H1	92	9	6	14 supplied separately	
	(Abridged Version)		44		6	6)	
1969	Exeter & District Joint Feasibility Study	LG/P2/H4	154	78	22	15 supplied separately	
	(Abridged Version)		43	9	8	8)	
1969	County Development Plan Second Review						
	Analysis of Survey	LG/P2/H3	119	104		11	
	Written Statement	LG/P1/H3	65				
1974	**Honiton Report – Adopted as ODP and Town Centre Plan**	LG/P1/H1	24		–	2	
1974	SWEPC *Strategic Settlement Pattern for the South West*	CG/P2/H4	24	2	–	4	
1975	*Towards 2001 – The Future of the Exeter Sub-Region*	LG/P2/H2	36	6	7	–	
1977	Structure Plan – Report of Survey	LG/P2/H3	184	87	23	39	2,500
	The Structural Options	LG/P2/H3	134	23	11	–	1,000
1978	Draft Written Statement	LG/P2/H3	272	56	19	–	2,500
1979	**Written Statement**	LG/P1/H3	196	66	19	–	4,000
	* * * * * * * * * *						
	Following approval by the Secretary of State, the Written Statement with modifications was published						
1981	Structure Plan — Written Statement		212	69	19	–	3,000

THE DOCUMENTATION — SOME INDICATION OF THE PRACTICAL TASK INVOLVED

The *Honiton Feasibility Study* of 1968 draw on the advice and expertise of officers in almost 20 institutions or undertakings, most of them government bodies or nationalised industries. The list of those whose assistance is acknowledged included, apart from the planning staff directly responsible, ten senior officers of Devon County Council and three of Honiton Municipal Borough Council, plus officers of the Greater London Council, the Devon and Exeter Executive Council for the Health Services, the Exeter and Mid-Devon Hospital Management Committee, the South Western Regional Hospital Board, the Devon River Authority, the Devon and Cornwall Constabulary, the Ministry of Agriculture, Fisheries and Food, the Ministry of Defence, the Ministry of Labour, the General Post Office, British Rail Western Region, the East Devon Water Board, the South Western Gas Board, the South Western Electricity Board, Exeter University, the National Farmers Union, and the Devon General Omnibus Company.

The 92-page study was accompanied by 14 maps, and a 38-page abridged version was also published with six maps. The report made a meticulous study of the existing condition of the town. It listed the acreage of neighbouring woodlands, and commented on the architectural and historic interest of the fabric of the town, its function as a centre for shopping, agricultural services, employment and social, cultural and recreational life. It listed the statutory services available (fire, police, library etc.) and the existing communications by road, rail and (at Exeter) air. It noted the surrounding landscape quality with an Area of Outstanding Natural Beauty to south and east, and one of Great Landscape Value to east and north. It analysed the population and age structure, and the trends in employment. A careful study was made of the quality of surrounding agricultural land, and detailed statistics were produced on cropping patterns for the nearest 13 parishes. In addition, investigations were made of the number and type of holdings in the area, the system of tenure, the farm sizes in Honiton and the 13 parishes compared with wider local areas, with Devon, and with England and Wales as a whole, with an appendix giving further details such as the ages of the agricultural labour force and the number and type of animals sold in Honiton market. A special industrial enquiry was set up, with which all firms employing five or more workers assisted. An appendix listed each type of business, analysed its growth or decline over five years and the proportion of women employed; and compared the results with those for Devon and for Great Britain. A total of 178 employees were found to be engaged in manufacturing firms of the necessary size in Honiton and these were analysed by level of skill. Markets, sources of raw material, and methods of transport were investigated.

The following year, 1969, saw the publication of the *Exeter and District Joint Feasibility Study*, which ran to 154 pages plus an abridged report and a portfolio of 18 maps. This study ranged east to Sidmouth and Honiton, north beyond Tiverton, west into the Dartmoor National Park, and back to the coast beyond Dawlish and Teignmouth, covering two municipal boroughs, seven urban districts, and four rural districts. The study was conducted jointly with Exeter City Council (then a County Borough). In addition to the project director and the liaison officer between the two authorities, 11 planning officers were engaged upon the study, which also drew on the help of seven other (non-planning) officers both from Devon County Council and of Exeter City Council, plus assistance from town clerks and planning officers in 16 local authorities, counties, cities or boroughs in England, Scotland and Wales, four water boards, 15 ministries or statutory undertakings, five educational institutions, and some four miscellaneous bodies such as local sports clubs. It was, in short, very comprehensive, examining every aspect of the physical, demographic, economic, and social environment, with searching appendices on such matters as travel patterns, industry and employment, farm sizes, ownership and crop patterns, entertainment and sports facilities in all the towns of the area (including, e.g. botanical gardens, bingo halls, rifle ranges, discotheques etc.) and comparing them with facilities in nine cities of southern England, such as Salisbury and Winchester. There were 22 full pages of sketches and diagrams.

Towards 2001, the Exeter sub-regional study of 1975, was a less ambitious document than its 1968 predecessor, the *Exeter and District Joint Feasibility Study*, but even so it involved consultations with the Gas and Electricity Boards, the Regional Health Authority, the South West Water Authority, the Ministry of Agriculture, the Department of the Environment, and representatives of manufacturers and of local estate agents. In recent years preparation of these studies has included the pre-publication involvement of local officers and councillors in varying permutations and combinations. Work on the Exeter sub-regional study, for instance, drew in representatives of Exeter, East Devon, Tiverton and Teignbridge District Councils, and observers from Torbay were also welcomed. Almost four years of anxious consultation preceded the publication of SWEPC's 1975 *Strategic Settlement Pattern*. Even more extensive consultation has succeeded publication, with Honiton and other councillors, for instance, attending discussion sessions in Exeter, and travelling to Bristol to discuss SWEPC reports.

Within two years, in 1977, the *Report of Survey* for the Structure Plan was ready, and 2,500 copies were published. It was much more comprehensive than the *Analysis of Survey* which had preceded production of each of the old County Development Plans; indeed it was a veritable domesday book, running to 184 close packed pages. It was accompanied by 41 maps beginning with areas of landscape importance, and proceeding via demonstrations of population change to refuse disposal facilities and major strategic movements of all vehicles on a typical August weekday in 1975, ending with military training areas and housing land requirements. There were 23 figures, ranging from age structure by districts over unemployment levels to national forecasts of car ownership. There were 87 tables dealing with such matters as housing condition and tenure, the ratio of private office floorspace to population in 1971 in the major urban centres, the production and export of ball clay, 1968–74, the ownership, management and species of woodland in 1965, and the estimated spending power of Devon residents in 1991, broken down by Economic Planning Area. Much of this information, the Introduction explained, would be up-dated annually by means of a series of surveys relating to the settlement pattern and employment; primary industries; urban conservation; recreation and rural conservation; and holiday development. Thus it would be possible to maintain continuous monitoring of the plan.

Out of this massive *tour de'horizon* a consultation paper was evolved on *The Structural Options and Draft Policies/Proposals*. Some 1,000 copies were made available. It covered five options for the absorption of the then – current expected increase in population, and worked out, for each option, the implications in terms of employment, land, transport, drainage and sewerage; and each option is accompanied by a table of settlements showing what the implications would be in terms of the settlement's function, land needs and changes of infrastructure. The following 42 organisations or officers were approached for their technical evaluations:

Comments received from

Agriculture   Ministry of Agriculture, Fisheries & Food

113

Employment	County Estates Surveyor
	Department of Industry
	Department of Employment
	Development Commission
Transportation	Department of Transport
	British Rail
	National Travel (South West Ltd.)
	County Engineer
Water Supply & Drainage	South West Water Authority
Other Utility Services	South Western Gas Board
	South Western Electricity Board
	P.O. Telecommunications (S.W. Region)
County Council Services	Social Services
	Education
Health Services	Devon Area Health Authority
Other County Councils	Somerset
	Cornwall
Other Consultees	Dartmoor, National Park Office
	Defence Land Agency
	Department of the Environment
Housing	The Housing Corporation
	All District Councils (apart from Exeter)
	(nine districts)

Response, but no comments, from

National Ports Council
Devon Fire Brigade
Devon & Cornwall Constabulary
Department of Education & Science

No response by December 1977

Civil Aviation Authority
National Water Council
Central Electricity Generating Board
S.W. Regional Health Authority
County Library Service
Exeter City Council Housing Dept.
Dorset County Council

The next stage, the *Draft Written Statement*, of which 2,500 copies were printed, ran to 272 pages, with 18 supporting diagrams and a detachable key diagram in a wallet at the back. In addition to policies for five areas selected for "major change", 137 general policies were promulgated. The lion's share, 41 in all, concerned transportation, and ranged from specific lists of proposed road schemes to more general if somewhat unilluminating pronouncements such as ensuring "that the necessary means of access to sea ports is provided according to their county and regional importance whilst having due regard to the environment of the surrounding area."

In November 1979, after five years of intense involvement at all local authority levels, and with the advice and participation of all statutory undertakings and various public and private associations and pressure groups in Devon, the Structure Plan was approved by Devon County Council. It ran to nearly 200 printed pages with 19 diagrams and 66 tables; some 4,000 copies were printed. In March 1980 the Secretary of State's public examination of the proposals began. In April 1981 it was approved by the

Secretary of State with various modifications. The final Devon County Structure Plan contained 212 pages and included 19 diagrams and 69 tables. Three thousand copies were printed.